# KETO DIET FOR WOMEN OVER 50

The Complete Guide for Beginners to Lose Weight Fast Following the Revolutionary Ketogenic Diet.

200+ Tastiest and Easiest Recipes and a 28 Day Meal Plan

D1604554

# Sommario

# Introduction

So the Ketogenic Diet is all about reducing the amount of carbohydrates you eat. Does this mean you won't get the kind of energy you need for the day? Of course not! It only means that now, your body has to find other possible sources of energy. Do you know where they will be getting that energy? Your stored body fat! This means it is NOT LOSING FAT, but rather, it is transforming your body into a fat burning machine. Nothing can be more boring than waiting for the weight to drop because it's just so hard to find a good workout plan that would help you with losing fat, right? Wrong! Ketogenic Diet simply requires you to have a very low carbohydrate diet. The whole program is built around examining your daily eating habits and finding any signs of unhealthy eating habits. It will help you find the best way to modify your habits and eat only what's good for you. The diet works if you want it to and that's why ketogenic diet program is so popular! It helps you examine your wrong eating habits and modify them in the right way. You will have the opportunity to try it yourself in just a few days, isn't that great? You won't have to wait more than that to see the results. But how can it work in the long run? It is said to be a healthy, sustainable and long term lifestyle. You get to eat your favorite foods in a simple way and you get to choose how you meet your daily nutrition needs.

So now that you know how to hack ketosis, write down your current carb intake, and how many grams of fibre you consume, let's get to the good stuff. In the guide to ketosis, we have designed a step-by-step diet for beginners that will effectively get your body into ketosis relatively quickly:

This low-carb diet plan is based on one that was used by early Native American hunters. It is different from the keto diet you may be used to. Although both have a bit of protein, this one is focused on eating more vegetables, healthy fats and fresh foods. According to the website, it is "a minimum of 60-80% greens, legumes, vegetables, herbs and spices. The idea is that these foods are low in digestible carbohydrates and rich in nutrients."

So here's the situation – you are eating less carbohydrates every day. To keep you energetic, the body breaks down the stored fat and turns them into molecules called ketone bodies. The process of turning the fat into ketone bodies is called "Ketosis" and obviously – this is where the name of the Ketogenic Diet comes from. The ketone bodies take the place of glucose in keeping you energetic. As long as you keep your carbohydrates reduced, the body will keep getting its energy from your body fat.

The Ketogenic Diet is often praised for its simplicity and when you look at it properly, the process is really straightforward. The Science behind the effectivity of the diet is also well-documented, and has been proven multiple times by different medical fields. For example, an article on Diet Review by Harvard provided a lengthy discussion on how the Ketogenic Diet works and why it is so effective for those who choose to use this diet.

# Is the Keto Diet Healthy for People Over 50?

The health benefits of the Keto diet are not different for men or women, but the speed at which they are reached does differ. As mentioned, human bodies are a lot different when it comes to the ways that they are able to burn fats and lose weight. For example, by design women have at least 10% more body fat than men. No matter how fit you are, this is just an aspect of being a human that you must consider. Don't be hard on yourself if you notice that it seems like men can lose weight easier that's because they can! What women have in additional body fat, men typically have the same in muscle mass. This is why men tend to see faster external results, because that added muscle mass means that their metabolism rates are higher. That increased metabolism means that fat and energy get burned faster. When you are on Keto, though, the internal change is happening right away.

Your metabolism is unique, but it is also going to be slower than a man's by nature. Since muscle is able to burn more calories than fat, the weight just seems to fall off of men, giving them the ability to reach the opportunity for muscle growth quickly. This should not be something that holds you back from starting your Keto journey. As long as you are keeping these realistic bodily factors in mind, you won't be left wondering why it is taking you a little bit longer to start losing weight. This point will come for you, but it will take a little bit more of a process that you must be committed to following through with.

Another unique condition that a woman can experience but a man cannot be PCOS or Polycystic Ovary Syndrome; a hormonal imbalance that causes the development of cysts. These cysts can cause pain, interfere with normal reproductive function, and, in extreme and dangerous cases, burst. PCOS is actually very common among women, affecting up to 10% of the entire female population. Surprisingly, most women are not even aware that they have the condition. Around 70% of women have PCOS that is undiagnosed. This condition can cause a significant hormonal imbalance, therefore affecting your metabolism. It can also inevitably lead to weight gain, making it even harder to see results while following diet plans. In order to stay on top of your health, you must make sure that you are going to the gynecologist regularly.

Menopause is another reality that must be faced by women, especially as we age. Most women begin the process of menopause in their mid-40s. Men do not go through menopause, so they are spared from yet another condition that causes slower metabolism and weight gain. When you start menopause, it is easy to gain weight and lose muscle. Most women, once menopause begins, lose muscle at a much faster rate, and conversely gain weight, despite dieting and exercise regimens.

Keto can, therefore, be the right diet plan for you. Regardless of what your body is doing naturally, via processes like menopause, your internal systems are still going to be making the switch from running on carbs to deriving energy from fats.

When the body begins to run on fats successfully, you have an automatic fuel reserving waiting to be burned. It will take some time for your body to do this, but when it does, you will actually be able to eat fewer calories and still feel just as full because your body knows to take energy from the fat that you already have. This will become automatic. It is, however, a process that requires some patience, but being aware of what is actually going on with your body can help you stay motivated while on Keto.

Because a Keto diet reduces the amount of sugar you are consuming, it naturally lowers the amount of insulin in your bloodstream. This can actually have amazing effects on any existing PCOS and fertility issues, as well as menopausal symptoms and conditions like pre-diabetes and Type 2 diabetes. Once your body adjusts to a Keto diet, you are overcoming the things that are naturally in place that can be preventing you from losing weight and getting healthy. Even if you placed your body on a strict diet, if it isn't getting rid of sugars properly, you likely aren't going to see the same results that you will when you try Keto. This is a big reason why Keto can be so beneficial for women.

You might not even realize that your hormones are not in balance until you experience a lifestyle that limits carbs and eliminates sugars. Keto is going to reset this balance for you, keeping your hormones at healthy levels. As a result of this, you will probably find yourself in a better general mood, and with much more energy to get through your days.

For people over 50, there are guidelines to follow when you start your Keto diet. As long as you are following the method properly and listening to what your body truly needs, you should have no more problems than men do while following the plan. What you will have are more obstacles to overcome, but you can do it. Remember that plenty of women successfully follow a Keto diet and see great results. Use these women as inspiration for how you anticipate your own journey to go. On the days when it seems impossible, remember what you have working against you, but more importantly what you have working for you. Your body is designed to go into ketogenesis more than it is designed to store fat by overeating carbs. Use this as a motivation to keep pushing you ahead. Keto is a valid option for you and the results will prove this, especially if you are over the age of 50.

# The Keto Mistakes Everyone Makes

Do you feel like you are giving your all to the Keto diet but you still aren't seeing the results you want? You are measuring ketones, working out, and counting your macros, but you still aren't losing the weight you want. Here are the most common mistakes that most people make when beginning the Keto diet.

## 1. Too Many Snacks

There are many snacks you can enjoy while following the Keto diet, like nuts, avocado, seeds, and cheese. But, snacking can be an easy way to get too many calories into the diet while giving your body an easy fuel source besides stored fat. Snacks need to be only used if you frequently hunger between meals. If you aren't extremely hungry, let your body turn to your stored fat for its fuel between meals instead of dietary fat.

## 2. Not Consuming Enough Fat

The ketogenic diet isn't all about low carbs. It's also about high fats. You need to be getting about 75 percent of your calories from healthy fats, five percent from carbs, and 20 percent from protein. Fat makes you feel fuller longer, so if you eat the correct amount, you will minimize your carb cravings, and this will help you stay in ketosis. This will help your body burn fat faster.

## 3. Consuming Excessive Calories

You may hear people say you can eat what you want on the Keto diet as long as it is high in fat. Even though we want that to be true, it is very misleading. Healthy fats need to make up the biggest part of your diet. If you eat more calories than what you are burning, you will gain weight, no matter what you eat because these excess calories get stored as fat. An average adult only needs about 2,000 calories each day, but this will vary based on many factors like activity level, height, and gender.

## 4. Consuming a lot of Dairies

For many people, dairy can cause inflammation and keeps them from losing weight. Dairy is a combo food meaning it has carbs, protein, and fats. If you eat a lot of cheese as a snack for the fat content, you are also getting a dose of carbs and protein with that fat. Many people can tolerate dairy, but moderation is the key. Stick with no more than one to two ounces of cheese or cream at each meal. Remember to factor in the protein content.

## 5. Consuming a lot of Protein

The biggest mistake that most people make when just beginning the Keto diet is consuming too much protein. Excess protein gets converted into glucose in the body called gluconeogenesis. This is a natural process where the body converts the energy from fats and proteins into glucose when glucose isn't available. When following a ketogenic diet, gluconeogenesis happens at different rates to keep body function. Our bodies don't need a lot of carbs, but we do need glucose. You can eat absolute zero carbs, and through gluconeogenesis, your body will convert other substances into glucose to be used as fuel. This is why carbs only make up five percent of your macros. Some parts of our bodies need carbs to survive, like kidney, medulla, and red blood cells. With gluconeogenesis, our bodies make and stores extra glucose as glycogen just in case supplies become too low.

In a normal diet, when carbs are always available, gluconeogenesis happens slowly because the need for glucose is extremely low. Our body runs on glucose and will store excess protein and carbs as fat.

## 6. Not Getting Enough Water

Water is crucial for your body. Water is needed for all your body does, and this includes burning fat. If you don't drink enough water, it can cause your metabolism to slow down, and this can halt your weight loss. Drinking 64 ounces or one-half gallon every day will help your body burn fat, flush out toxins, and circulate nutrients. When you are just beginning the Keto diet, you might need to drink more water since your body will begin to get rid of body fat by flushing it out through urine.

## 7. Consuming Too Many Sweets

Some people might indulge in Keto brownies and Keto cookies that are full of sugar substitute just because their net carb content is low, but you have to remember that you are still eating calories. Eating sweets might increase your carb cravings. Keto sweets are great on occasion; they don't need to be a staple in the diet.

## 8. Not Getting Enough Sleep

Getting plenty of sleep is needed in order to lose weight effectively. Without the right amount of sleep, your body will feel stressed, and this could result in your metabolism slowing down. It might cause it to store fat instead of burning fat. When you feel tired, you are more tempted to drink more lattes for energy, eat a snack to give you an extra boost, or order takeout rather than cooking a healthy meal. Try to get between seven and nine hours of sleep each night. Understand that your body uses that time to burn fat without you even lifting a finger.

## 9. Low on Electrolytes

Most people will experience the Keto flu when you begin this diet. This happens for two reasons when your body changes from burning carbs to burning fat, your brain might not have enough energy, and this, in turn, can cause grogginess, headaches, and nausea. You could be dehydrated, and your electrolytes might be low since the Keto diet causes you to urinate often.

Getting the Keto flu is a great sign that you are heading in the right direction. You can lessen these symptoms by drinking more water or taking supplements that will balance your electrolytes.

## 10. Consuming Hidden Carbs

Many foods look like they are low carb, but they aren't. You can find carbs in salad dressings, sauces, and condiments. Be sure to check nutrition labels before you try new foods to make sure it doesn't have any hidden sugar or carbs. It just takes a few seconds to skim the label, and it might be the difference between whether or not you'll lose weight.

If you have successfully ruled out all of the above, but you still aren't losing weight, you might need to talk with your doctor to make sure you don't have any health problems that could be preventing your weight loss. This can be frustrating, but stick with it, stay positive, and stay in the game. When the Keto diet is done correctly, it is one of the best ways to lose weight.

# How to Get into Ketosis

### Ketogenic Vs Low Carb

Keto and low carbohydrate diets are similar in many ways. On a ketogenic diet, the body moves to a ketosis state, and the brain is ultimately powered by ketones. These are produced in the liver when the intake of carbohydrates is very small. Low carbohydrate diets may entail diverse things for different people. Low-carb diets actually reduce your overall carbohydrate consumption.

For regular low-carb diets, brain habits are still mostly glucose-dependent, although they may consume higher ketones than standard diets. To accomplish this, you'd have to follow low-carb, low-calorie, and an active lifestyle. The amount of carbohydrate you eat depends on the type of diet you consume.

At the end of the day, low carb is reduced in your carb intake. Mentions can vary enormously depending on the number of total carbs consumed per day. People have different views and follow different rules, from 0 to 100 grams of net carbs. Though a ketogenic diet has low carbohydrates, it also has significantly low protein levels. The overall increase in blood levels of ketones is significant.

### What Is Ketosis?

When you reduce the intake of carbs over a period of time, the body can begin to break down body fat for energy for daily tasks. This is a natural occurrence called ketosis that the body undergoes to help us survive while food intake is small. We create ketones during this process, produced from the breakdown of fats in the liver. Once ketones are processed into energy, they are a byproduct of fatty acids.

Blood ketone bodies also increase substantially to higher than normal levels. Mind, muscle and all tissue that includes mitochondria utilize ketones. With practice, you'll soon learn how to understand ketosis signs.

A properly controlled ketogenic diet has the function of pushing your body into the metabolic state to consume fats as energy. Not by depriving the body of calories but by eliminating sugars. The bodies are outstandingly resilient to what you place in them. Taking keto nutrients such as keto OS can improve cell regeneration, strength, and lifespan. If an excess of fats is available, and carbs are eliminated, ketones can continue to burn as the primary source of energy.

### Can A Keto Diet Help You Lose Weight?

There are different ways that a ketogenic diet will help a person shed excess fat in their body to meet their target weight. Scientists are still doing thorough research to understand just how this whole process works and how precisely the condition of ketosis helps an individual in terms of losing their excess weight.

Because protein intake is improved in most situations when a person moves to a ketogenic diet, and there are many healthy eating choices, including some veggies, that are filled with fiber in this specific type of diet, one of the most popular reasons would be better satiety. For fiber and protein, you'll find that you don't feel hungry as long as you've had a meal similar to before you had such same meals and you've decided to follow the diet.

With improved satiety and dieting plans, binge eating is something that can usually be avoided effectively. If you don't feel hungry between the main meals of the day, there's little need for a bag of potato chips or an energy bar.

Nonetheless, there would be moments where hunger hits–in such situations, carrying a handful of nuts can be a very healthy alternative to those energy bars, donuts, and other unhealthy, dangerous snacks that you normally choose when you find you need to consume when it's not time for the following meal.

# Foods Allowed in Keto Diet

To make the most of your diet, there are prohibited foods, and others that are allowed, but in limited quantities. Here are the foods allowed in the ketogenic diet:

## Food allowed in unlimited quantities

### Lean or fatty meats

No matter which meat you choose, it contains no carbohydrates so that you can have fun! Pay attention to the quality of your meat, and the amount of fat. Alternate between fatty meats and lean meats!

Here are some examples of lean meats:

Beef: sirloin steak, roast beef, 5% minced steak, roast, flank steak, tenderloin, Grisons meat, tripe, kidneys

Horse: roti, steak

Pork: tenderloin, bacon, kidneys

Veal: cutlet, shank, tenderloin, sweetbread, liver

Chicken and turkey: cutlet, skinless thigh, ham

Rabbit

Here are some examples of fatty meats:

Lamb: leg, ribs, brain

Beef: minced steak 10, 15, 20%, ribs, rib steak, tongue, marrow

Pork: ribs, brain, dry ham, black pudding, white pudding, bacon, terrine, rillettes, salami, sausage, sausages, and merguez

Veal: roast, paupiette, marrow, brain, tongue, dumplings

Chicken and turkey: thigh with skin

Guinea fowl

Capon

Turkey

Goose: foie gras

### Lean or fatty fish

The fish does not contain carbohydrates so that you can consume unlimited! As with meat, there are lean fish and fatty fish, pay attention to the amount of fat you eat and remember to vary your intake of fish. Oily fish have the advantage of containing a lot of good cholesterol, so it is beneficial for protection against cardiovascular disease! It will be advisable to consume fatty fish more than lean fish, to be able to manage your protein intake: if you consume lean fish, you will have a significant protein intake and little lipids, whereas with fatty fish, you will have a balanced protein and fat intake!

Here are some examples of lean fish:

- Cod
- Colin
- Sea bream
- Whiting
- Sole
- Turbot
- Limor career
- Location
- Pike
- Ray

Here are some examples of oily fish:

- Swordfish
- Salmon
- Tuna
- Trout
- Monkfish
- Herring
- Mackerel
- Cod
- Sardine

Eggs

The eggs contain no carbohydrates, so you can consume as much as you want. It is often said that eggs are full of cholesterol and that you have to limit their intake, but the more cholesterol you eat, the less your body will produce by itself! In addition, it's not just poor-quality cholesterol so that you can consume 6 per week without risk! And if you want to eat more but you are afraid for your cholesterol and I have not convinced you, remove the yellow!

## Vegetables and raw vegetables

Yes, you can eat vegetables.  But you have to be careful which ones: you can eat leafy vegetables (salad, spinach, kale, red cabbage, Chinese cabbage...) and flower vegetables (cauliflower, broccoli, Romanesco cabbage...) as well as avocado, cucumbers, zucchini or leeks, which do not contain many carbohydrates.

## The oils

It's oil, so it's only fat, so it's unlimited to eat, but choose your oil wisely! Prefer olive oil, rapeseed, nuts, sunflower or sesame for example!

## Foods authorized in moderate quantities.

### The cold cuts

As you know, there is bad cholesterol in cold meats, so you will need to moderate your intake: eat it occasionally!

### Fresh cheeses and plain yogurts

Consume with moderation because they contain carbohydrates.

### Nuts and oilseeds

They have low levels of carbohydrates, but are rich in saturated fatty acids, that's why they should moderate their consumption. Choose almonds, hazelnuts, Brazil nuts or pecans.

### Coconut (in oil, cream or milk)

It contains saturated fatty acids, that's why we limit its consumption. Cream and coconut oil contain a lot of medium chain triglycerides (MCTs), which increase the level of ketones, essential to stay in ketosis.

### Berries and red fruits

They contain carbohydrates, in reasonable quantities, but you should not abuse them to avoid ketosis (blueberries, blackberries, raspberries...).

# Benefit of Keto Diet for People Over 50

**Benefits Ketogenic Diet**

**Reduction of cravings and appetite**

Many people gain weight simply because they cannot control their cravings and appetite for caloric foods. The ketogenic diet helps eliminate these problems, but it does not mean that you will never be hungry or want to eat. You will feel hungry but only when you have to eat. Several studies have shown that the less carbohydrates you eat, the less you eat overall. Eating healthier foods that are high in fat helps reduce your appetite, as you lose more weight faster on a low-fat diet. The reason for this is that low carbohydrate diets help lower insulin levels, as your body does not need too much insulin to convert glycogen to glucose while eliminating excess water in your body. This diet helps you reduce visceral fat. In this way, you will get a slimmer look and shape. It is the most difficult fat to lose, as it surrounds the organs as it increases. High doses can cause inflammation and insulin resistance. Coconut oil can produce an immediate source of energy as it increases ketone levels in your body.

**Reduction of risk of heart disease**

Triglycerides, fat molecules in your body, have close links with heart disease. They are directly proportional as the more the number of triglycerides, the higher your chances of suffering from heart disease. You can reduce the number of free triglycerides in your body by reducing the number of carbohydrates, as is in the keto diets.

**Reduces chances of having high blood pressure**

Weight loss and blood pressure have a close connection; thus, since you are losing weight while on the keto diet, it will affect your blood pressure.

**Fights type 2 diabetes**

Type two diabetes develops as a result of insulin resistance. This is a result of having huge amounts of glucose in your system, with the keto diet this is not a possibility due to the low carbohydrate intake.

**Increases the production of HDL**

High-density lipoprotein is referred to as good cholesterol. It is responsible for caring calories to your liver, thus can be reused. High fat and low carbohydrate diets increase the production of HDL in your body, which also reduces your chances of getting a heart disease. Low-density lipoprotein is referred to as bad cholesterol.

## Suppresses your appetite

It is a strange but true effect of the keto diet. It was thought that this was a result of the production of ketones but this was proven wrong as a study taken between people on a regular balanced diet and some on the keto diet and their appetites were generally the same. It, however, helps to suppress appetite as it is it has a higher fat content than many other diets. Food stays in the stomach for longer as fat and is digested slowly, thus provides a sense of fullness. On top of that, proteins promote the secretion cholecystokinin, which is a hormone that aids in regulating appetite. It is also believed that the ketogenic diet helps to suppress your appetite by continuous blunting of appetite. There is increased appetite in the initial stages of the diet, which decreases over time.

## Changes in cholesterol levels

This is kind of on the fence between good and bad. This is because the ketogenic diet involves a high fat intake which makes people wonder about the effect on blood lipids and its potential to increase chances of heart disease and strokes, among others. Several major components play a lead role in determining this, which is: LDL, HDL, and blood triglyceride levels. Heart disease correlates with high levels of LDL and cholesterol. On the other hand, high levels of HDL are seen as protection from diseases caused by cholesterol levels. The impacts of the diet on cholesterol are not properly known. Some research has shown that there is no change in cholesterol levels while others have said that there is change. If you stay in deep ketosis for a very long period of time, your blood lipids will increase, but you will have to go through some negative effects of the ketogenic diet which will be corrected when the diet is over. If a person does not remain following the diet strictly for like ten years, he/she will not experience any cholesterol problems. It is difficult to differentiate the difference between diet and weight loss in general. The effect of the ketogenic diet on cholesterol has been boiled down to if you lose fat on the ketogenic diet then your cholesterol levels will go down, and if you don't lose fat, then your cholesterol levels will go up. Strangely, women have a larger cholesterol level addition than men, while both are on a diet. As there is no absolute conclusion on the effect of the ketogenic diet on cholesterol, you are advised to have your blood lipid levels constantly checked for any bad effects. Blood lipid levels should be checked before starting the diet and about eight weeks after starting. If repeated results show a worsening of lipid levels, then you should abandon the diet or substitute saturated fats with unsaturated fats.

## Risk of a Ketogenic Diet

## Low energy levels

When available, the body prefers to use carbohydrates for fuel as they burn more effectively than fats. General drop-in energy level is a concern raised by many dieters due to the lack of carbohydrates. Studies have shown that it causes orthostatic hypotension which causes lightheadedness. It has come to be known that these effects can be avoided by providing enough supplemental nutrients like sodium. Many of the symptoms can be prevented by providing 5 grams of sodium per day. Most times, fatigue disappears after a few weeks or even days, if fatigue doesn't disappear, then you should add a small number of carbohydrates to the diet as long as ketosis is maintained. The diet is not recommended when caring out high-intensity workouts, weight training, or high-intensity aerobic exercise as carbohydrates are an absolute requirement but are okay for low-intensity exercise.

## Effects on the brain

It causes increased use of ketones by the brain. The increased use of ketones, among other reasons, result in the treating of childhood epilepsy. As a result of the changes that occur, the concern over the side effects, including permanent brain damage and short-term memory loss, has been raised. The origin of these concerns is difficult to understand. The brain is powered by ketones in the absence of glucose. Ketones are normal energy sources and not toxic as the brain creates enzymes, during fetal growth, that helps us use them. Epileptic children, though not the perfect examples, show some insight into the effects of the diet on the brain in the long term. There is no negative effect in terms of cognitive function. There is no assurance that the diet cannot have long term dietary effects, but no information proves that there are any negative effects. Some people feel they can concentrate more when on the ketogenic diet, while others feel nothing but fatigue. This is as a result of differences in individual physiology. There are very few studies that vaguely address the point on short term memory loss. This wore off with the continuation of the study.

## Kidney stones and kidney damage

As a result of the increased workload from having to filter ketones, urea, and ammonia, as well as dehydration concerns of the potential for kidney damage or passing kidney stones have been raised. The high protein nature of the ketogenic diet raises the alarms of individuals who are concerned with potential kidney damage. There is very little information that points to any negative effects of the diet on kidney function or development of kidney stones. There is a low incidence of small kidney stones in epileptic children this may be as a result of the state of deliberate dehydration that the children are put at instead of the ketosis state itself. Some short term research shows no change in kidney function or increased incidents of kidney stones either after they are off the diet or after six months on a diet. There is no long term data on the effects of ketosis to kidney function; thus, no complete conclusions can be made. People with preexisting kidney issues are the only ones who get problems from high protein intake. From an unscientific point of view, one would expect increased incidents of this to happen to athletes who consume very high protein diets, but it has not happened. This suggests that high protein intake, under normal conditions, is not harmful to the kidneys. To limit the possibility of kidney stones, it is advised to drink a lot of water to maintain hydration. For people who are predisposed to kidney stones should have their kidney function should be monitored to ensure that no complications arise if they decide to follow through with the diet.

## Constipation

A common side effect of the diet is reduced bowel movements and constipation. This arises from two different causes: lack of fiber and gastrointestinal absorption of foods. First, the lack of carbs in the diet means that unless supplements are taken, fiber intake is low. Fiber is very important to our systems. High fiber intake can prevent some health conditions, including heart disease and some forms of cancer. Use some type of sugar-free fiber supplement to prevent any health problems and help you maintain regular bowel movements. The diet also reduces the volume of stool due to enhanced absorption and digestion of food; thus, fewer waste products are generated.

## Fat regain

Dieting, in general, has very low long term success rates. There are some effects of getting out of a ketogenic diet like the regain of fat lost through calorific restriction alone. This is true for any diet based on calorific restriction. It is expected for weight to be regained after carb reintroduction. For people who use the weighing scale to measure their success, they may completely shun carbs as they think it is the main reason for the weight regain. You should understand that most of the initial weight gain is water and glycogen.

## Immune system

There is a large variety in the immunity system response to ketogenic diets on different people. There has been some repost on reduction on some ailments such allergies and increased minor sickness susceptibility.

## Optic neuropathy

This is optic nerve dysfunction. It has appeared in a few cases, but it is still existence. It was linked to the people not getting adequate amounts of calcium or vitamins supplements for about a year. All the cases were corrected by supplementation of adequate vitamin B, especially thiamine.

# Keto Grocery List

I've had people complain about the difficulty of switching their grocery list to one that's Ketogenic-friendly. The fact is that food is expensive – and most of the food you have in your fridge are probably packed full with carbohydrates. This is why if you're committing to a Ketogenic Diet, you need to do a clean sweep. That's right – everything that's packed with carbohydrates should be identified and set aside to make sure you're not eating more than you should. You can donate them to a charity before going out and buying your new Keto-friendly shopping list.

## Seafood

Seafood means fish like sardines, mackerel, and wild salmon. It's also a good idea to add some shrimp, tuna, mussels, and crab into your diet. This is going to be a tad expensive but definitely worth it in the long run. What's the common denominator in all these food items? The secret is omega-3 fatty acids which is credited for lots of health benefits. You want to add food rich in omega-3 fatty acids in your diet.

## Low-carb Vegetables

Not all vegetables are good for you when it comes to the Ketogenic Diet. The vegetable choices should be limited to those with low carbohydrate counts. Pack up your cart with items like spinach, eggplant, arugula, broccoli, and cauliflower. You can also put in bell peppers, cabbage, celery, kale, Brussels sprouts, mushrooms, zucchini, and fennel.

So what's in them? Well, aside from the fact that they're low-carb, these vegetable also contain loads of fiber which makes digestion easier. Of course, there's also the presence of vitamins, minerals, antioxidants, and various other nutrients that you need for day to day life. Which ones should you avoid? Steer clear of the starch-packed vegetables like carrots, turnips, and beets. As a rule, you go for the vegetables that are green and leafy.

## Fruits Low in Sugar

During an episode of sugar-craving, it's usually a good idea to pick low-sugar fruit items. Believe it or not, there are lots of those in the market! Just make sure to stock up on any of these: avocado, blackberries, raspberries, strawberries, blueberries, lime, lemon, and coconut. Also note that tomatoes are fruits too so feel free to make side dishes or dips with loads of tomatoes! Keep in mind that these fruits should be eaten fresh and not out of a can. If you do eat them fresh off the can however, take a good look at the nutritional information at the back of the packaging. Avocadoes are particularly popular for those practicing the Ketogenic Diet because they contains LOTS of the good kind of fat.

## Meat and Eggs

While some diets will tell you to skip the meat, the Ketogenic Diet actually encourages its consumption. Meat is packed with protein that will feed your muscles and give you a consistent source of energy through the day. It's a slow but sure burn when you eat protein as opposed to carbohydrates which are burned faster and therefore stored faster if you don't use them immediately.

But what kind of meat should you be eating? There's chicken, beef, pork, venison, turkey, and lamb. Keep in mind that quality plays a huge role here – you should be eating grass-fed organic beef or organic poultry if you want to make the most out of this food variety. The organic option lets you limit the possibility of ingesting toxins in your body due to the production process of these products. Plus, the preservation process also means there are added salt or sugar in the meat, which can throw off the whole diet.

## Nuts and Seeds

Nuts and seeds you should definitely add in your cart include: chia seeds, Brazil nuts, macadamia nuts, flaxseed, walnuts, hemp seeds, pecans, sesame seeds, almonds, hazelnut, and pumpkin seeds. They also contain lots of protein and very little sugar so they're great if you have the munchies. They're the ideal snack because they're quick, easy, and will keep you full. They're high in calories though, which is why lots of people steer clear of them. As I mentioned earlier though – the Ketogenic Diet has nothing to do with calories and everything to do with the nutrient you're eating. So don't pay too much attention on the calorie count and just remember that they're a good source of fats and protein.

## Dairy Products

OK – some people in their 50s already have a hard time processing dairy products, but for those who don't – you can happily add many of these to your diet. Make sure to consume sufficient amounts of cheese, plain Greek yogurt, cream butter, and cottage cheese. These dairy products are packed with calcium, protein, and the healthy kind of fat.

## Oils

Nope, we're not talking about essentials oils but rather, MCT oil, coconut oil, avocado oil, nut oils, and even extra-virgin olive oil. You can start using those for your frying needs to create healthier food options. The beauty of these oils is that they add flavor to the food, making sure you don't get bored quickly with the recipes. Try picking up different types of Keto-friendly oils to add some variety to your cooking.

## Coffee and Tea

The good news is that you don't have to skip coffee if you're going on a Ketogenic Diet. The bad news is that you can't go to Starbucks anymore and order their blended coffee choices. Instead, beverages would be limited to unsweetened tea or unsweetened coffee in order to keep the sugar consumption low. Opt for organic coffee and tea products to make the most out of these powerful antioxidants.

## Dark Chocolate

Yes – chocolate is still on the menu, but it is limited to just dark chocolate. Technically, this means eating chocolate that is 70 percent cacao, which would make the taste a bit bitter.

## Sugar Substitutes

Later in the recipes part of this book, you might be surprised at some of the ingredients required in the list. This is because while sweeteners are an important part of food preparation, you can't just use any kind of sugar in your recipe. Remember: the typical sugar is pure carbohydrate. Even if you're not eating carbohydrates, if you're dumping lots of sugar in your food – you're not really following the Ketogenic Diet principles.

So what do you do? You find sugar substitutes. The good news is that there are LOTS of those in the market. You can get rid of the old sugar and use any of these as a good substitute.

Stevia. This is perhaps the most familiar one in this list. It's a natural sweetener derived from plants and contains very few calories. Unlike your typical sugar, stevia may actually help lower the sugar levels instead of causing it to spike. Note though that it's sweeter than actual sugar so when cooking with stevia, you'll need to lower the amount used. Typically, the ratio is 200 grams of sugar per 1 teaspoon of powdered stevia.

Sucralose. It contains zero calories and zero carbohydrates. It's actually an artificial sweetener and does not metabolize – hence the complete lack of carbohydrates. Splenda is actually a sweetener derived from sucralose. Note though that you don't want to use this as a baking substitute for sugar. Its best use is for coffee, yogurt, and oatmeal sweetening. Note though that like stevia, it's also very sweet – in fact, it's actually 600 times sweeter than the typical sugar. Use sparingly.

Erythritol. It's a naturally occurring compound that interacts with the tongue's sweet taste receptors. Hence, it mimics the taste of sugar without actually being sugar. It does contain calories, but only about 5% of the calories you'll find in the typical sugar. Note though that it doesn't dissolve very well so anything prepared with this sweetener will have a gritty feeling. This can be problematic if you're using the product for baking. As for sweetness, the typical ratio is 1 1/3 cup for 1 cup of sugar.

Xylitol. Like erythritol, xylitol is a type of sugar alcohol that's commonly used in sugar-free gum. While it still contains calories, the calories are just 3 per gram. It's a sweetener that's good for diabetic patients because it doesn't raise the sugar levels or insulin in the body. The great thing about this is that you don't have to do any computations when using it for baking, cooking, or fixing a drink. The ratio of it with sugar is 1 to 1 so you can quickly make the substitution in the recipe.

What about Condiments?

Condiments are still on the table, but they won't be as tasty as you're used to. Your options include mustard, olive oil mayonnaise, oil-based salad dressings, and unsweetened ketchup. Of all these condiments, ketchup is the one with the most sugar, so make a point of looking for one with reduced sugar content. Or maybe avoid ketchup altogether and stick to mustard?

What about Snacks?

The good news is that there are packed snacks for those who don't have the time to make it themselves. Sugarless nut butters, dried seaweeds, nuts, and sugar-free jerky are all available in stores. The nuts and seeds discussed in a previous paragraph all make for excellent snack options.

What about Labels?

Let's not fool ourselves into thinking that we can cook food every single day. The fact is that there will be days when there will be purchases for the sake of convenience. There are also instances when you'll have problems finding the right ingredients for a given recipe. Hence, you'll need to find substitutes for certain ingredients without losing the "Keto friendly" vibe of the product.

So what should be done? Well, you need to learn how to read labels. Food doesn't have to be specially made to be keto-friendly, you just have to make sure that it doesn't contain any of the unfriendly nutrients or that the carbohydrate content is low enough.

# 28 Days Meal Plan

| Days | Breakfast | Lunch | Dinner | Snacks |
|------|-----------|-------|--------|--------|
| 1 | Antipasti Skewers | Buttered Cod | Beef-Stuffed Mushrooms | Blueberry Scones |
| 2 | Kale, Edamame and Tofu Curry | Salmon with Red Curry Sauce | Rib Roast | Homemade Graham Crackers |
| 3 | Chocolate Cupcakes with Matcha Icing | Salmon Teriyaki | Beef Stir Fry | Buffalo Chicken Sausage Balls |
| 4 | Sesame Chicken Salad | Pesto Shrimp with Zucchini Noodles | Sweet & Sour Pork | Brussels Sprouts Chips |
| 5 | Jalapeno Poppers | Crab Cakes | Grilled Pork with Salsa | Keto Chocolate Mousse |
| 6 | BLT Party Bites | Tuna Salad | Garlic Pork Loin | Keto Berry Mousse |
| 7 | Strawberries and Cream Smoothie | Keto Frosty | Chicken Pesto | Peanut Butter Mousse |
| 8 | Cauli Flitters | Keto Shake | Garlic Parmesan Chicken Wings | Cookie Ice Cream |
| 9 | Bacon Wrapped Chicken Breast | Keto Fat Bombs | Crispy Baked Shrimp | Mocha Ice Cream |

| | | | |
|---|---|---|---|
| 10 | No-Bake Keto Power Bars | Avocado Ice Pops | Herbed Mediterranean Fish Fillet | Raspberry Cream Fat Bombs |
| 11 | Avocado Toast | Carrot Balls | Mushroom Stuffed with Ricotta | Cauliflower Tartar Bread |
| 12 | Almond Flour Pancakes | Coconut Crack Bars | Thai Chopped Salad | Buttery Skillet Flatbread |
| 13 | Chicken Avocado Egg Bacon Salad | Buttered Cod | Lemon & Rosemary Salmon | Fluffy Bites |
| 14 | Keto Flu Combat Smoothie | Strawberry Ice Cream | Chicken Kurma | Coconut Fudge |
| 15 | Bacon Hash | Key Lime Pudding | Pork Chops with Bacon & Mushrooms | Nutmeg Nougat |
| 16 | Egg Salad | Chicken, Bacon and Avocado Cloud Sandwiches | Pork | Sweet Almond Bites |
| 17 | Bagels with Cheese | Roasted Lemon Chicken Sandwich | Garlic Shrimp | Strawberry Cheesecake Minis |
| 18 | Capicola Egg Cups | Keto-Friendly Skillet Pepperoni Pizza | Pork Chop | Cocoa Brownies |

| 19 | Scrambled Eggs | Cheesy Chicken Cauliflower | Citrus Egg Salad | Blueberry Scones |
|---|---|---|---|---|
| 20 | Frittata with Spinach | Chicken Soup | Chowder | Homemade Graham Crackers |
| 21 | Cheese Omelet | Chicken Avocado Salad | Beef-Stuffed Mushrooms | Buffalo Chicken Sausage Balls |
| 22 | Antipasti Skewers | Chicken Broccoli Dinner | Rib Roast | Brussels Sprouts Chips |
| 23 | Kale, Edamame and Tofu Curry | Easy Meatballs | Beef Stir Fry | Keto Chocolate Mousse |
| 24 | Chocolate Cupcakes with Matcha Icing | Chicken Casserole | Sweet & Sour Pork | Keto Berry Mousse |
| 25 | Sesame Chicken Salad | Lemon Baked Salmon | Grilled Pork with Salsa | Peanut Butter Mousse |
| 26 | Jalapeno Poppers | Italian Sausage Stacks | Garlic Pork Loin | Cookie Ice Cream |
| 27 | BLT Party Bites | Baked Salmon | Chicken Pesto | Mocha Ice Cream |
| 28 | Strawberries and Cream Smoothie | Tuna Patties | Garlic Parmesan | Raspberry Cream Fat Bombs |

|  |  |  | Chicken Wings |  |
|--|--|--|--|--|

# Breakfast

**Antipasti Skewers**

**Preparation Time: 10 minutes**

**Cooking Time: 0 minute**

**Servings: 6**

**Ingredients:**

- 6 small mozzarella balls
- 1 tablespoon olive oil
- Salt to taste
- 1/8 teaspoon dried oregano
- 2 roasted yellow peppers, sliced into strips and rolled
- 6 cherry tomatoes
- 6 green olives, pitted
- 6 Kalamata olives, pitted
- 2 artichoke hearts, sliced into wedges
- 6 slices salami, rolled
- 6 leaves fresh basil

**Directions:**

1. Toss the mozzarella balls in olive oil.
2. Season with salt and oregano.
3. Thread the mozzarella balls and the rest of the ingredients into skewers.
4. Serve in a platter.

**Nutrition:**

Calories 180

Total Fat 11.8g

Saturated Fat 4.5g

Cholesterol 26mg

Sodium 482mg

Total Carbohydrate 11.7g

Dietary Fiber 4.8g

Total Sugars 4.1g

Protein 9.2g

Potassium 538mg

## Kale, Edamame and Tofu Curry

**Preparation Time: 20 minutes**

**Cooking Time: 40 minutes**

**Servings: 3**

**Ingredients:**

- 1 tablespoon rapeseed oil
- 1 large onion, chopped
- Four cloves garlic, peeled and grated
- 1 large thumb (7cm) fresh ginger, peeled and grated
- 1 red chili, deseeded and thinly sliced
- 1/2 teaspoon ground turmeric
- 1/4 teaspoon cayenne pepper
- 1 teaspoon paprika
- 1/2 teaspoon ground cumin
- 1 teaspoon salt
- 250 g / 9 oz. dried red lentils
- 1-liter boiling water
- 50 g / 1.7 oz. frozen soya beans
- 200 g / 7 oz. firm tofu, chopped into cubes
- Two tomatoes, roughly chopped
- Juice of 1 lime
- 200 g / 7 oz. kale leaves stalk removed and torn

## Directions:

1. Put the oil in a pan over low heat. Add your onion and cook for 5 minutes before adding the garlic, ginger, and chili and cooking for a further 2 minutes. Add your turmeric, cayenne, paprika, cumin, and salt and Stir through before adding the red lentils and stirring again.
2. Pour in the boiling water and allow it to simmer for 10 minutes, reduce the heat and cook for about 20-30 minutes until the curry has a thick '•porridge' consistency.
3. Add your tomatoes, tofu and soya beans and cook for a further 5 minutes. Add your kale leaves and lime juice and cook until the kale is just tender.

## Nutrition:

Calories 133

Carbohydrate 54

Protein 43

## Chocolate Cupcakes with Matcha Icing
## Preparation Time: 35 minutes

## Cooking Time: 0 minutes

## Servings: 4

## Ingredients:

- 150g / 5 oz. self-rising flour
- 200 g / 7 oz. caster sugar
- 60 g / 2.1 oz. cocoa
- ½ teaspoon. salt
- ½ teaspoon. fine espresso coffee, decaf if preferred
- 120 ml / ½ cup milk
- ½ teaspoon. vanilla extract
- 50 ml / ¼ cup vegetable oil
- 1 egg
- 120 ml / ½ cup of water
- For the icing:
- 50 g / 1.7 oz. butter,
- 50 g / 1.7 oz. icing sugar
- 1 tablespoon matcha green tea powder

- ½ teaspoon vanilla bean paste
- 50 g / 1.7 oz. soft cream cheese

**Directions**:

1. Heat the oven and Line a cupcake tin with paper
2. Put the flour, sugar, cocoa, salt, and coffee powder in a large bowl and mix well.
3. Add milk, vanilla extract, vegetable oil, and egg to dry ingredients and use an electric mixer to beat until well combined. Gently pour the boiling water slowly and beat on low speed until completely combined. Use the high speed to beat for another minute to add air to the dough. The dough is much more liquid than a normal cake mix. Have faith; It will taste fantastic!
4. Arrange the dough evenly between the cake boxes. Each cake box must not be more than ¾ full. Bake for 15-18 minutes, until the dough resumes when hit. Remove from oven and allow cooling completely before icing.
5. To make the icing, beat your butter and icing sugar until they turn pale and smooth. Add the matcha powder and vanilla and mix again. Add the cream cheese and beat until it is smooth. Pipe or spread on the cakes.

**Nutrition:**

calories435

Fat 5

Fiber 3

Carbs 7

Protein 9

## Sesame Chicken Salad

**Preparation Time: 20 minutes**

**Cooking Time: 0 minutes**

**Servings: 4**

**Ingredients:**

- 1 tablespoon of sesame seeds
- 1 cucumber, peeled, halved lengthwise, without a teaspoon, and sliced.
- 100 g / 3.5 oz. cabbage, chopped
- 60 g pak choi, finely chopped
- ½ red onion, thinly sliced
- Large parsley (20 g / 0.7 oz.), chopped.
- 150 g / 5 oz. cooked chicken, minced
- For the dressing:
- 1 tablespoon of extra virgin olive oil
- 1 teaspoon of sesame oil
- 1 lime juice
- 1 teaspoon of light honey
- 2 teaspoons soy sauce

**Directions:**

1. Roast your sesame seeds in a dry pan for 2 minutes until they become slightly golden and fragrant.
2. Transfer to a plate to cool.
3. In a small bowl, mix olive oil, sesame oil, lime juice, honey, and soy sauce to prepare the dressing.

4. Place the cucumber, black cabbage, pak choi, red onion, and parsley in a large bowl and mix gently.
5. Pour over the dressing and mix again.
6. Distribute the salad between two dishes and complete with the shredded chicken. Sprinkle with sesame seeds just before serving.

## Nutrition:

Calories 345

Fat 5

Fiber 2

Carbs 10

Protein 4

## Jalapeno Poppers

**Preparation Time: 30 minutes**

**Cooking Time: 60 minutes**

**Servings: 10**

**Ingredients:**

- 5 fresh jalapenos, sliced and seeded
- 4 oz. package cream cheese
- ¼ lb. bacon, sliced in half

**Directions:**

1. Preheat your oven to 275 degrees F.
2. Place a wire rack over your baking sheet.
3. Stuff each jalapeno with cream cheese and wrap in bacon.
4. Secure with a toothpick.
5. Place on the baking sheet.
6. Bake for 1 hour and 15 minutes.

**Nutrition:**

Calories 103

Total Fat 8.7g

Saturated Fat 4.1g

Cholesterol 25mg

Sodium 296mg

Total Carbohydrate 0.9g

Dietary Fiber 0.2g

Total Sugars 0.3g

Protein 5.2g

Potassium 93mg

**BLT Party Bites**

**Preparation Time: 35 minutes**

**Cooking Time: 0 minute**

**Servings: 8**

**Ingredients:**

- 4 oz. bacon, chopped
- 3 tablespoons panko breadcrumbs
- 1 tablespoon Parmesan cheese, grated
- 1 teaspoon mayonnaise
- 1 teaspoon lemon juice
- Salt to taste
- ½ heart Romaine lettuce, shredded
- 6 cocktail tomatoes

**Directions**:

1. Put the bacon in a pan over medium heat.
2. Fry until crispy.
3. Transfer bacon to a plate lined with paper towel.
4. Add breadcrumbs and cook until crunchy.
5. Transfer breadcrumbs to another plate also lined with paper towel.
6. Sprinkle Parmesan cheese on top of the breadcrumbs.
7. Mix the mayonnaise, salt and lemon juice.
8. Toss the Romaine in the mayo mixture.
9. Slice each tomato on the bottom to create a flat surface so it can stand by itself.
10. Slice the top off as well.
11. Scoop out the insides of the tomatoes.

12. Stuff each tomato with the bacon, Parmesan, breadcrumbs and top with the lettuce.

## Nutrition:

Calories 107

Total Fat 6.5g

Saturated Fat 2.1g

Cholesterol 16mg

Sodium 360mg

Total Carbohydrate 5.4g

Dietary Fiber 1.5g

Total Sugars 3.3g

Protein 6.5g

Potassium 372mg

# Strawberries and Cream Smoothie

**Preparation Time**: 5 minutes

**Cooking Time**: 15 minutes

**Servings**: 1

**Ingredients:**

- 5 medium strawberries, hulled
- 3 tablespoons heavy (whipping) cream
- 3 ice cubes
- Your favorite vanilla-flavored sweetener

**Directions:**

1.In a blender, combine all the ingredients and blend until smooth. Enjoy right away!

**Nutrition:**

Calories: 176

Total Fat: 16g

Protein: 2g

Total Carbs: 6g

Fiber: 1g

Net Carbs: 5g

**Cauli Flitters**

**Preparation Time: 10 minutes**

**Cooking Time: 15 minutes**

**Servings: 2**

**Ingredients:**

- 2 eggs
- 1 head of cauliflower
- 1 tbsp. yeast
- sea salt, black pepper
- 1-2 tbsp. ghee
- 1 tbsp. turmeric
- 2/3 cup almond flour

**Directions:**

1. Place the cauliflower into a large pot and start to boil it for 8 mins. Add the florets into a food processor and pulse them.
2. Add the eggs, almond flour, yeast, turmeric, salt and pepper to a mixing bowl. Stir well. Form into patties.
3. Heat your ghee to medium in a skillet. Form your fritters and cook until golden on each side (3-4 mins).
4. Serve it while hot.

**Nutrition:**

Calories: 238 kcal

Fat: 23 g

Carbs: 5 g

Protein: 6 g

**Bacon Wrapped Chicken Breast**

**Preparation Time: 10 minutes**

**Cooking Time: 45 minutes**

**Servings: 4**

**Ingredients**

- 4 boneless, skinless chicken breast
- 8 oz. sharp cheddar cheese
- 8 slices bacon
- 4 oz. sliced jalapeno peppers
- 1 tsp garlic powder
- Salt and pepper to taste

**Directions**

1. Preheat the oven at around 3500F. Ensure to season both sides of chicken breast well with salt, garlic powder, and pepper. Place the chicken breast on a non-stick baking sheet (foil-covered). Cover the chicken with cheese and add jalapeno slices. Cut the bacon slices in half and then place the four halves over each piece of chicken. Bake for around 30 to 45 minutes at most. If the chicken is set but the bacon still feels undercooked, you may want to put it under the broiler for a few minutes. Once done, serve hot with a side of low carb garlic parmesan roasted asparagus.

**Nutrition:**

Calories: 640

Fat: 48g

Carbohydrates: 6g

Fiber: 3g

Net carbs: 3g

Protein: 47g

## No-Bake Keto Power Bars

**Preparation Time**: 10 Minutes plus Overnight to Chill

**Cooking Time**: 20 minutes

**Servings**: 12 bars

### Ingredients:

- ½ cup pili nuts
- ½ cup whole hazelnuts
- ½ cup walnut halves
- ¼ cup hulled sunflower seeds
- ¼ cup unsweetened coconut flakes or chips
- ¼ cup hulled hemp seeds
- 2 tablespoons unsweetened cacao nibs
- 2 scoops collagen powder (I use 1 scoop Perfect Keto vanilla collagen and 1 scoop Perfect Keto unflavored collagen powder)
- ½ teaspoon ground cinnamon
- ½ teaspoon sea salt
- ¼ cup coconut oil, melted
- 1 teaspoon vanilla extract
- Stevia or monk fruit to sweeten (optional if you are using unflavored collagen powder)

### Directions:

1. Line a 9-inch square baking pan with parchment paper.

2. In a food processor or blender, combine the pili nuts, hazelnuts, walnuts, sunflower seeds, coconut, hemp seeds, cacao nibs, collagen powder, cinnamon, and salt and pulse a few times.

3. Add the coconut oil, vanilla extract, and sweetener (if using). Pulse again until the ingredients are combined. Do not over pulse or it will turn to mush. You want the nuts and seeds to have some texture still.

4. Pour the mixture into the prepared pan and press it into an even layer. Cover with another piece of parchment (or fold over extra from the first piece) and place a heavy pan or dish on top to help press the bars together.

5. Refrigerate overnight and then cut into 12 bars. Store the bars in individual storage bags in the refrigerator for a quick grab-and-go breakfast.

## Nutrition:

Calories: 242

Total Fat: 22g

Protein: 6.5g

Total Carbs: 4.5g

Fiber: 2.5g

Net Carbs: 2g

**Avocado Toast**

**Preparation Time: 20 minutes**

**Cooking Time: 40 minutes**

**Servings: 2**

**Ingredients**

- ½ cup grass-fed butter
- 2 tbsp coconut oil
- 7 large eggs
- 1 tsp baking powder
- 2 cups almond flour
- ½ tsp xanthan gum
- ½ tsp kosher salt
- 1 medium avocado

**Directions**

1. Preheat over at 3500F. Beat eggs for around two minutes with a mixer at high speed. Then, add coconut oil and butter (both melted) to the eggs and continue beating. Ensure that oil and butter are not too warm to cook the eggs. Add remaining bread ingredients and mix well. Now, the batter should become thick. Pour batter in a non-stick loaf pan lined with parchment paper. Let it bake for 45 minutes or until the fork comes clean through the middle.
2. For topping, toast two slices of your keto bread to your liking. Slice the whole avocado thinly, without the skin or pit. Use these to make one long strip of

overlapping slices. Roll these into a spiral and that is it! Enjoy your keto bread with avocado topping.

## Nutrition:

Calories: 350

Fat: 32g

Carbohydrates: 7g

Fiber: 4g

Net carbs: 3g

Protein: 10g

## Almond Flour Pancakes

## Preparation Time: 5 minutes

## Cooking Time: 5 minutes

## Servings: 4

## Ingredients

- ½ cup almond flour
- ½ cup cream cheese
- 4 medium eggs
- ½ tsp cinnamon
- ½ tsp granulated sweetener
- 1 tsp grass-fed butter
- 1 tbsp sugar-free syrup

## Directions

1. Add all the ingredients into a blender and let them blend in well. Once done, set the batter aside.
2. On a non-stick pan at medium heat, fry pancakes with melted butter. Once the center starts to bubble, turn over. Once done with the pancake, move on to the rest, using the batter.
3. Finally, serve your pancakes warm, along with some low carb fruit or with an exquisite side of sugar-free syrup to enjoy a healthy and tasty breakfast.

## Nutrition:

Calories: 234                                   Protein: 11g

Fat: 20g

Carbohydrates: 4g

Fiber: 1.5g

Net carbs: 2.5g

**Chicken Avocado Egg Bacon Salad**

**Preparation Time: 10 minutes**

**Cooking Time: 10 minutes**

**Servings: 4**

**Ingredients**

- 12 oz. cooked chicken breast
- 6 slices crumbled bacon
- 3 boiled eggs cut into cubes
- 1 cup cherry tomatoes cut into halves
- 1/2 small sliced red onion
- 1 large avocado(s)
- 1/2 stick finely chopped celery
- Salad Dressing
- 1/2 cup olive oil mayonnaise
- 2 tbsp. sour cream
- 1 tsp Dijon mustard
- 4 tbsp. extra virgin olive oil
- 2 cloves minced garlic
- 2 tsp lemon juice
- 4 cups lettuce
- Salt and pepper to taste

## Directions

1. Combine all the ingredients together and mix them well for the salad dressing. Then, combine chicken, tomatoes, bacon, eggs, red onions, and celery together. Add about ¾ of the salad dressing and mix them well. Add the avocado and toss together gently. Check the taste and, if needed, add the remainder of the salad dressing as well. Finally, add salt and pepper to taste and then serve it over lettuce.

## Nutrition:

Calories: 387

Fat: 27g

Carbohydrates: 2.5g

Fiber: 1g

Net carbs: 1.5g

Protein: 24g

## Keto Flu Combat Smoothie

**Preparation Time**: 5 Minutes

**Cooking Time**: 15 minutes

**Servings**: 1

**Ingredients:**

- ½ cup unsweetened nut or seed milk (hemp, almond, coconut, and cashew)
- 1 cup spinach
- ½ medium avocado (about 75 grams), pitted and peeled
- 1 scoop MCT powder (or 1 tablespoon MCT oil)
- ½ tablespoon unsweetened cacao powder
- ¼ teaspoon of sea salt

- Dash sweetener (optional)
- ½ cup ice

## Directions:

1. In a blender, combine the milk, spinach, avocado, MCT powder, cacao powder, salt, sweetener (if using), and ice and blend until smooth.

## Nutrition:

Calories: 249

Total Fat: 21g

Protein: 5g

Total Carbs: 10g

Fiber: 8g

Net Carbs: 2g

## Bacon Hash

## Preparation Time: 5 minutes

## Cooking Time: 10 minutes

## Servings: 2

## Ingredients:

- Small green pepper ( 1)
- Jalapenos (2)
- Small onion (1)
- Eggs (4)
- Bacon slices (6)

## Directions:

1. Chop the bacon into chunks using a food processor. Set aside for now. Slice the onions and peppers into thin strips. Dice the jalapenos as small as possible.

2. Heat a skillet and fry the veggies. Once browned, combine the fixings and cook until crispy. Place on a serving dish with the eggs.

## Nutrition:

Carbohydrates: 9 grams

Calories: 366

Protein: 23 grams

Fats: 24 grams

**Egg Salad**

**Preparation Time: 15 minutes**

**Cooking Time: 10 minutes**

**Servings: 4**

**Ingredients**

- 6 eggs
- 2 tbsp mayonnaise
- 1 tsp Dijon mustard
- 1 tsp lemon juice
- Salt and pepper to taste

**Directions**

1. In a medium saucepan, place the solid eggs gently.
2. Add some cold water so that the eggs are covered around an inch. Boil them for around 10 minutes.

3. Once done, remove them from the heat and let them cool. Peel the eggs while running them under cold water. Now add these in a food processor and pulse until they are chopped.
4. Add and stir mayonnaise, lemon juice, mustard, and salt and pepper. Ensure to taste and then adjust as necessary.
5. Finally, serve them with a bit of lettuce leaves and, if needed, bacon for wrapping.

## Nutrition:

Calories: 222

Fat: 19g

Net carbs: 1g

Protein: 13g

**Bagels with Cheese**

**Preparation Time: 10 minutes**

**Cooking Time: 15 minutes**

**Servings: 6**

**Ingredients:**

- Mozzarella cheese (2.5 cups)
- Baking powder (1 tsp.)
- Cream cheese (3 oz.)
- Almond flour (1.5 cups)
- Eggs (2)

**Directions:**

1. Shred the mozzarella and combine with the flour, baking powder, and cream cheese in a mixing container. Pop into the microwave for about one minute. Mix well.
2. Let the mixture cool and add the eggs. Break apart into six sections and shape into round bagels. Note: You can also sprinkle with a seasoning of your choice or pinch of salt if desired.
3. Bake them for approximately 12 to 15 minutes. Serve or cool and store.

## Nutrition:

Carbohydrates: 8 grams

Protein: 19 grams

Fats: 31 grams

Calories: 374

**Capicola Egg Cups**

**Preparation Time: 5 minutes**

**Cooking Time: 15 minutes**

**Servings: 4**

**Ingredients:**

- 8 eggs
- 1 cup cheddar cheese
- 4 oz. capicola or bacon (slices)
- salt, pepper, basil

**Directions:**

1. Preheat the oven to 400°F. You will need 8 wells of a standard-size muffin pan.
2. Place the slices in the 8 wells, forming a cup shape. Sprinkle into each cup some of the cheese, according to your liking.
3. Crack an egg into each cup, season them with salt and pepper.
4. Bake for 10-15 mins. Serve hot, top it with basil.

**Nutrition**:

Carbs: 1 g

Fat: 11 g

Protein: 16 g

Calories: 171 kcal

**Scrambled Eggs**

**Preparation Time: 2 minutes**

**Cooking Time: 8 minutes**

**Servings: 4**

**Ingredients:**

- 4 oz. butter
- 8 eggs
- salt and pepper for taste

**Directions:**

1. Crack the eggs in a bowl, and whisk them together, while seasoning it.
2. Melt the butter in a skillet over medium heat, but don't turn it into brown.
3. Pour the eggs into the skillet and cook it for 1-2 mins, until they look and feel fluffy and creamy.
4. Tip: If you want to shake things up, you can pair this one up with bacon, salmon, or maybe avocado as well.

**Nutrition:**

Carbs: 1 g

Fat: 31 g

Protein: 11 g

Calories: 327 kcal

**Frittata with Spinach**

**Preparation Time: 5 minutes**

**Cooking Time: 30 minutes**

**Servings: 4**

**Ingredients**:

- 8 eggs
- 8 ozs. fresh spinach
- 5 ozs. diced bacon
- 5 ozs. shredded cheese
- 1 cup heavy whipping cream
- 2 tbsps. butter
- salt and pepper

**Directions:**

1. Preheat the oven to 350 °F
2. Fry the bacon until crispy, add the spinach and cook until wilted. Set them aside.
3. Whisk the cream and eggs together, and pour it into the baking dish.
4. Add the cheese, spinach, and bacon on the top, and place in the oven. Bake for 25-30 minutes, until golden brown on top.

**Nutrition:**

Carbs: 4 g

Fat: 59 g

Protein: 27 g

Calories: 661 kcal

## Cheese Omelet

**Preparation Time: 5 minutes**

**Cooking Time: 10 minutes**

**Servings: 2**

**Ingredients:**

- 6 eggs
- 3 ozs. ghee
- 7 ozs. shredded cheddar cheese
- salt and pepper

**Directions:**

1. Whisk the eggs until smooth. Compound half of the cheese and season it with salt and pepper.
2. Melt the butter in a pan. Pour in the mixture and let it sit for a few minutes (3-4)
3. When the mixture is looking good, add the other half of the cheese. Serve immediately.

**Nutrition:**

Carbs: 4 g

Fat: 80 g

Protein: 40 g

Calories: 897 kcal

# Lunch

**Buttered Cod**

**Preparation Time:** 5 minutes

**Cooking Time:** 5 minutes

**Servings:** 4

**Ingredients:**

- 1 ½ lb. cod fillets, sliced
- 6 tablespoons butter, sliced
- ¼ teaspoon garlic powder
- ¾ teaspoon ground paprika
- Salt and pepper to taste
- Lemon slices
- Chopped parsley

**Directions:**

1. Mix the garlic powder, paprika, salt and pepper in a bowl.
2. Season cod pieces with seasoning mixture.
3. Add 2 tablespoons butter in a pan over medium heat.
4. Let half of the butter melt.
5. Add the cod and cook for 2 minutes per side.
6. Top with the remaining slices of butter.
7. Cook for 3 to 4 minutes.
8. Garnish with parsley and lemon slices before serving.

**Nutrition:**

Calories 295

Total Fat 19g

Saturated Fat 11g

Cholesterol 128mg

Sodium 236mg

Total Carbohydrate 1.5g

Dietary Fiber 0.7g

Total Sugars 0.3g

Protein 30.7g

Potassium 102mg

## Salmon with Red Curry Sauce

**Preparation Time:** 10 minutes

**Cooking Time:** 22 minutes

**Servings:** 4

**Ingredients:**

- 4 salmon fillets
- 2 tablespoons olive oil
- Salt and pepper to taste
- 1 ½ tablespoons red curry paste
- 1 tablespoon fresh ginger, chopped
- 14 oz. coconut cream
- 1 ½ tablespoons fish sauce

**Directions:**

1. Preheat your oven to 350 degrees F.
2. Cover baking sheet with foil.
3. Brush both sides of salmon fillets with olive oil and season with salt and pepper.
4. Place the salmon fillets on the baking sheet.
5. Bake salmon in the oven for 20 minutes.
6. In a pan over medium heat, mix the curry paste, ginger, coconut cream and fish sauce.
7. Sprinkle with salt and pepper.
8. Simmer for 2 minutes.
9. Pour the sauce over the salmon before serving.

## Nutrition:

Calories 553

Total Fat 43.4g

Saturated Fat 24.1g

Cholesterol 78mg

Sodium 908mg

Total Carbohydrate 7.9g

Dietary Fiber 2.4g

Total Sugars 3.6g

Protein 37.3g

Potassium 982mg

## Salmon Teriyaki

**Preparation Time:** 15 minutes

**Cooking Time:** 25 minutes

**Servings:** 6

**Ingredients:**

- 3 tablespoons sesame oil
- 2 teaspoons fish sauce
- 3 tablespoons coconut amino
- 2 teaspoons ginger, grated
- 4 cloves garlic, crushed
- 2 tablespoons xylitol
- 1 tablespoon green lime juice
- 2 teaspoons green lime zest
- Cayenne pepper to taste
- 6 salmon fillets
- 1 teaspoon arrowroot starch
- ¼ cup water
- Sesame seeds

**Directions:**

1. Preheat your oven to 400 degrees F.
2. Combine the sesame oil, fish sauce, coconut amino, ginger, garlic, xylitol, green lime juice, zest and cayenne pepper in a mixing bowl.

3. Create 6 packets using foil.
4. Add half of the marinade in the packets.
5. Add the salmon inside.
6. Place in the baking sheet and cook for about 20 to 25 minutes.
7. Add the remaining sauce in a pan over medium heat.
8. Dissolve arrowroot in water, and add to the sauce.
9. Simmer until the sauce has thickened.
10.     Place the salmon on a serving platter and pour the sauce on top.
11.     Sprinkle sesame seeds on top before serving.

**Nutrition:**

Calories 312

Total Fat 17.9g

Saturated Fat 2.6g

Cholesterol 78mg

Sodium 242mg

Total Carbohydrate 3.5g

Dietary Fiber 0.1g

Total Sugars 0.1g

Protein 34.8g

Potassium 706mg

# Pesto Shrimp with Zucchini Noodles

**Preparation Time:** 10 minutes

**Cooking Time:** 15 minutes

**Servings:** 3

**Ingredients:**

- Pesto sauce
- 3 cups basil leaves
- ¾ cup pine nuts
- 2 cloves garlic
- ½ lemon, juiced
- 1 teaspoon lemon zest
- Salt to taste
- ¼ cup olive oil
- Shrimp and Zoodles
- 3 zucchinis
- Salt to taste
- 1 lb. shrimp
- 2 tablespoons avocado oil

**Directions:**

1. Put all the pesto ingredients in a blender.
2. Blend until smooth.
3. Spiralize the zucchini into noodle form.
4. Season with salt.
5. Drain water from the zucchini noodles.
6. Season the shrimp with salt and pepper.
7. Add half of the oil in a pan over medium heat.
8. Once the oil is hot, add the shrimp and cook for 1 to 2 minutes.
9. Add the remaining oil to the pan.
10. Add the zucchini noodles and cook for 3 minutes.
11. Add the pesto and toss to coat the noodles evenly with the sauce.
12. Season with salt.

## Nutrition:

Calories 304

Total Fat 22.2g

Saturated Fat 2.6g

Cholesterol 159mg

Sodium 223mg

Total Carbohydrate 8g

Dietary Fiber 2.3g

Total Sugars 2.5g

Protein 21.3g

Potassium 547mg

## Crab Cakes

**Preparation Time:** 1 hour and 20 minutes

**Cooking Time:** 20 minutes

**Servings:** 8

**Ingredients:**

- 2 tablespoons butter
- 2 cloves garlic, minced
- ½ cup bell pepper, chopped
- 1 rib celery, chopped
- 1 shallot, chopped
- Salt and pepper to taste
- 2 tablespoons mayonnaise
- 1 egg, beaten
- 1 teaspoon mustard
- 1 tablespoon Worcestershire sauce
- 1 teaspoon hot sauce
- ½ cup Parmesan cheese, grated
- ½ cup pork rinds, crushed
- 1 lb. crabmeat
- 2 tablespoons olive oil

## Directions:

- Add the butter to the pan over medium heat.
- Add the garlic, bell pepper, celery, shallot, salt and pepper.
- Cook for 10 minutes.
- In a bowl, mix the mayo, egg, Worcestershire, mustard and hot sauce.
- Add the sautéed vegetables to this mixture.

- Mix well.
- Add the cheese and pork rind.
- Fold in the crabmeat.
- Line the baking sheet with foil.
- Create patties from the mixture.
- Place the patties on the baking sheet.
- Cover the baking sheet with foil.
- Refrigerate for 1 hour.
- Fry in olive oil in a pan over medium heat.
- Cook until crispy and golden brown.

## Nutrition:

Calories 150

Total Fat 9.2g

Saturated Fat 3.2g

Cholesterol 43mg

Sodium 601mg

Total Carbohydrate 10.8g

Dietary Fiber 0.5g

Total Sugars 4.6g

Protein 6.4g

Potassium 80mg

**Tuna Salad**

**Preparation Time:** 5 minutes

**Cooking Time:** 0 minute

**Servings:** 2

**Ingredients:**

- 1 cup tuna flakes

- 3 tablespoons mayonnaise
- 1 teaspoon onion flakes
- Salt and pepper to taste
- 3 cups Romaine lettuce

## Directions:

1. Mix the tuna flakes, mayonnaise, onion flakes, salt and pepper in a bowl.
2. Serve with lettuce.

## Nutrition:

Calories 130

Total Fat 7.8g

Saturated Fat 1.1g

Cholesterol 13mg

Sodium 206mg

Total Carbohydrate 8.5g

Dietary Fiber 0.6g

Total Sugars 2.6g

Protein 8.2g

Potassium 132mg

## Keto Frosty

**Preparation Time:** 45 minutes

**Cooking Time:** 0 minute

**Servings:** 4

## Ingredients:

- 1 ½ cups heavy whipping cream
- 2 tablespoons cocoa powder (unsweetened)
- 3 tablespoons Swerve

- 1 teaspoon pure vanilla extract
- Salt to taste

## Directions:

1. In a bowl, combine all the ingredients.
2. Use a hand mixer and beat until you see stiff peaks forming.
3. Place the mixture in a Ziploc bag.
4. Freeze for 35 minutes.
5. Serve in bowls or dishes.

## Nutrition:

Calories 164

Total Fat 17g

Saturated Fat 10.6g

Cholesterol 62mg

Sodium 56mg

Total Carbohydrate 2.9g

Dietary Fiber 0.8g

Total Sugars 0.2g

Protein 1.4g

Potassium 103mg

## Keto Shake

**Preparation Time:** 15 minutes

**Cooking Time:** 0 minute

Serving: 1

## Ingredients:

- ¾ cup almond milk
- ½ cup ice
- 2 tablespoons almond butter
- 2 tablespoons cocoa powder (unsweetened)

- 2 tablespoons Swerve
- 1 tablespoon chia seeds
- 2 tablespoons hemp seeds
- ½ tablespoon vanilla extract
- Salt to taste

## Directions:

1. Blend all the ingredients in a food processor.
2. Chill in the refrigerator before serving.

## Nutrition:

Calories 104

Potassium 159mg

Total Fat 9.5g

Saturated Fat 5.1g

Cholesterol 0mg

Sodium 24mg

Total Carbohydrate 3.6g

Dietary Fiber 1.4g

Total Sugars 1.1g

Protein 2.9g

## Keto Fat Bombs

**Preparation Time:** 30 minutes

**Cooking Time:** 0 minute

**Servings:** 10

## Ingredients:

- 8 tablespoons butter
- ¼ cup Swerve
- ½ teaspoon vanilla extract
- Salt to taste
- 2 cups almond flour
- 2/3 cup chocolate chips

## Directions:

1. In a bowl, beat the butter until fluffy.
2. Stir in the sugar, salt and vanilla.
3. Mix well.
4. Add the almond flour.
5. Fold in the chocolate chips.
6. Cover the bowl with cling wrap and refrigerate for 20 minutes.
7. Create balls from the dough.

## Nutrition:

Calories 176

Total Fat 15.2g

Saturated Fat 8.4g

Cholesterol 27mg

Sodium 92mg

Total Carbohydrate 12.9g

Dietary Fiber 1g

Total Sugars 10.8g

Protein 2.2g

Potassium 45mg

## Avocado Ice Pops

**Preparation Time:** 20 minutes

**Cooking Time:** 0 minute

**Servings:** 10

## Ingredients:

- 3 avocados
- ¼ cup lime juice
- 3 tablespoons Swerve
- ¾ cup coconut milk
- 1 tablespoon coconut oil

- 1 cup keto friendly chocolate

## Directions:

1. Add all the ingredients except the oil and chocolate in a blender.
2. Blend until smooth.
3. Pour the mixture into the popsicle mold.
4. Freeze overnight.
5. In a bowl, mix oil and chocolate chips.
6. Melt in the microwave. And then let cool.
7. Dunk the avocado popsicles into the chocolate before serving.

## Nutrition:

Calories 176

Total Fat 17.4g

Saturated Fat 7.5g

Cholesterol 0mg

Sodium 6mg

Total Carbohydrate 10.8g

Dietary Fiber 4.5g

Total Sugars 5.4g

Protein 1.6g

Potassium 341mg

# Carrot Balls

**Preparation Time:** 1 hour and 10 minutes

**Cooking Time:** 0 minute

**Servings:** 8

**Ingredients:**

- 8 oz. block cream cheese
- ¾ cup coconut flour
- ½ teaspoon pure vanilla extract
- 1 teaspoon stevia
- ¼ teaspoon ground nutmeg
- 1 teaspoon cinnamon
- 1 cup carrots, grated
- 1/2 cup pecans, chopped
- 1 cup coconut, shredded

**Directions:**

Use a hand mixer to beat the cream cheese, coconut flour, vanilla, stevia, nutmeg and cinnamon.

Fold in the carrots and pecans.

Form into balls.

Refrigerate for 1 hour.

Roll into shredded coconut before serving.

**Nutrition:**

Calories 390

Total Fat 35g

Saturated Fat 17g

Cholesterol 60mg

Sodium 202mg

Total Carbohydrate 17.2g

Dietary Fiber 7.8g

Total Sugars 6g

Protein 7.8g

Potassium 154mg

## Coconut Crack Bars

**Preparation Time:** 2 minutes

**Cooking Time:** 3 minutes

**Servings:** 20

**Ingredients:**

- 3 cups coconut flakes (unsweetened)
- 1 cup coconut oil
- ¼ cup maple syrup

**Directions:**

1. Line a baking sheet with parchment paper.
2. Put coconut in a bowl.
3. Add the oil and syrup.
4. Mix well.
5. Pour the mixture into the pan.
6. Refrigerate until firm.
7. Slice into bars before serving.

**Nutrition:**

Calories 147

Total Fat 14.9g

Saturated Fat 13g

Cholesterol 0mg

Sodium 3mg

Total Carbohydrate 4.5g

Dietary Fiber 1.1g

Total Sugars 3.1g

Protein 0.4g

Potassium 51mg

## Strawberry Ice Cream

**Preparation Time:** 1 hour and 20 minutes

**Cooking Time:** 0 minute

**Servings:** 4

**Ingredients:**

- 17 oz. coconut milk
- 16 oz. frozen strawberries
- ¾ cup Swerve
- ½ cup fresh strawberries

**Directions:**

1. Put all the ingredients except fresh strawberries in a blender.
2. Pulse until smooth.
3. Put the mixture in an ice cream maker.
4. Use ice cream maker according to directions.
5. Add the fresh strawberries a few minutes before the ice cream is done.
6. Freeze for 1 hour before serving.

**Nutrition:**

Calories 320

Total Fat 28.8g

Saturated Fat 25.5g

Cholesterol 0mg

Sodium 18mg

Total Carbohydrate 25.3g

Dietary Fiber 5.3g

Total Sugars 19.1g

Protein 2.9g

Potassium 344mg

## Key Lime Pudding

**Preparation Time:** 20 minutes

**Cooking Time:** 1 hour and 15 minutes

**Servings:** 2

**Ingredients:**

- 1 cup hot water
- 2/4 cup erythrytol syrup
- 6 drops stevia
- 1 teaspoon almond extract
- 1 teaspoon vanilla extract
- ¼ teaspoon Xanthan gum powder
- 2 ripe avocados, sliced
- 1 ½ oz. lime juice
- 3 tablespoons coconut oil
- Salt to taste

**Directions:**

1. Add water, erythritol, stevia, almond extract and vanilla extract to a pot.
2. Bring to a boil.
3. Simmer until the syrup has been reduced and has thickened.
4. Turn the heat off.
5. Add the gum powder.
6. Mix until thickened.
7. Add the avocado into a food processor.
8. Add the rest of the ingredients.
9. Pulse until smooth.
10. Place the mixture in ramekins.
11. Refrigerate for 1 hour.
12. Pour the syrup over the pudding before serving.

**Nutrition:**

Calories 299

Total Fat 29.8g

Saturated Fat 12.9g

Cholesterol 0mg

Sodium 47mg

Total Carbohydrate 9.7g

Dietary Fiber 6.8g

Total Sugars 0.8g

Protein 2g

Potassium 502mg

**Chicken, Bacon and Avocado Cloud Sandwiches**

**Preparation Time: 10 minutes**

**Cooking Time: 25 minutes**

**Servings: 6**

**Ingredients:**

- For cloud bread
- 3 large eggs
- 4 oz. cream cheese
- ½ tablespoon. ground psyllium husk powder
- ½ teaspoon baking powder
- A pinch of salt
- To assemble sandwich
- 6 slices of bacon, cooked and chopped
- 6 slices pepper Jack cheese
- ½ avocado, sliced

- 1 cup cooked chicken breasts, shredded
- 3 tablespoons. mayonnaise

**Directions**:

1. Preheat your oven to 300 degrees.
2. Prepare a baking sheet by lining it with parchment paper.
3. Separate the egg whites and egg yolks, and place into separate bowls.
4. Whisk the egg whites until very stiff. Set aside.
5. Combined egg yolks and cream cheese.
6. Add the psyllium husk powder and baking powder to the egg yolk mixture. Gently fold in.
7. Add the egg whites into the egg mixture and gently fold in.
8. Dollop the mixture onto the prepared baking sheet to create 12 cloud bread. Use a spatula to spread the circles around to form ½-inch thick pieces gently.
9. Bake for 25 minutes or until the tops are golden brown.
10. Allow the cloud bread to cool completely before serving. Can be refrigerated for up to 3 days of frozen for up to 3 months. If food prepping, place a layer of parchment paper between each bread slice to avoid having them getting stuck together. Simply toast in the oven for 5 minutes when it is time to serve.
11. To assemble sandwiches, place mayonnaise on one side of one cloud bread. Layer with the remaining sandwich ingredients and top with another slice of cloud bread.

**Nutrition:**

Calories: 333 kcal

Carbs: 5g

Fat: 26g

Protein: 19.9g

# Roasted Lemon Chicken Sandwich

**Preparation Time: 15 minutes**

**Cooking Time: 1 hour 30 minutes**

**Servings: 12**

**Ingredients**:

- 1 kg whole chicken
- 5 tablespoons. butter
- 1 lemon, cut into wedges
- 1 tablespoon. garlic powder
- Salt and pepper to taste
- 2 tablespoons. mayonnaise
- Keto-friendly bread

**Directions**:

1. Preheat the oven to 350 degrees F.
2. Grease a deep baking dish with butter.
3. Ensure that the chicken is patted dry and that the gizzards have been removed.
4. Combine the butter, garlic powder, salt and pepper.
5. Rub the entire chicken with it, including in the cavity.
6. Place the lemon and onion inside the chicken and place the chicken in the prepared baking dish.
7. Bake for about 1½ hours, depending on the size of the chicken.
8. Baste the chicken often with the drippings. If the drippings begin to dry, add water. The chicken is done when a thermometer, insert it into the thickest part

of the thigh reads 165 degrees F or when the clear juices run when the thickest part of the thigh is pierced.

9.  Allow the chicken to cool before slicing.
10. To assemble sandwich, shred some of the breast meat and mix with the mayonnaise. Place the mixture between the two bread slices.
11. To save the chicken, refrigerated for up to 5 days or freeze for up to 1 month.

## Nutrition:

Calories: 214 kcal

Carbs: 1.6 g

Fat: 11.8 g

Protein: 24.4 g.

## Keto-Friendly Skillet Pepperoni Pizza

## Preparation Time: 10 minutes

## Cooking Time: 6 minutes

## Servings: 4

## Ingredients:

For Crust

½ cup almond flour

½ teaspoon baking powder

8 large egg whites, whisked into stiff peaks

Salt and pepper to taste

Toppings

3 tablespoons. Unsweetened tomato sauce

½ cup shredded cheddar cheese

½ cup pepperoni

## Directions

Gently incorporate the almond flour into the egg whites. Ensure that no lumps remain.

Stir in the remaining crust ingredients.

Heat a nonstick skillet over medium heat. Spray with nonstick spray.

Pour the batter into the heated skillet to cover the bottom of the skillet.

Cover the skillet with a lid and cook the pizza crust to cook for about 4 minutes or until bubbles that appear on the top.

Flip the dough and add the toppings, starting with the tomato sauce and ending with the pepperoni

Cook the pizza for 2 more minutes.

Allow the pizza to cool slightly before serving.

Can be stored in the refrigerator for up to 5 days and frozen for up to 1 month.

## Nutrition:

Calories: 175 kcal

Carbs: 1.9 g

Fat: 12 g

Protein: 14.3 g.

**Cheesy Chicken Cauliflower**

**Preparation Time: 5 minutes**

**Cooking Time: 10 minutes**

**Servings: 4**

**Ingredients:**

- 2 cups cauliflower florets, chopped
- ½ cup red bell pepper, chopped
- 1 cup roasted chicken, shredded (Lunch Recipes: Roasted Lemon Chicken Sandwich)
- ¼ cup shredded cheddar cheese
- 1 tablespoon. butter
- 1 tablespoon. sour cream
- Salt and pepper to taste

**Directions**:

1. Stir fry the cauliflower and peppers in the butter over medium heat until the veggies are tender.
2. Add the chicken and cook until the chicken is warmed through.
3. Add the remaining ingredients and stir until the cheese is melted.
4. Serve warm.

**Nutrition:**

Calories: 144 kcal

Carbs: 4 g

Fat: 8.5 g

Protein: 13.2 g.

**Chicken Soup**

**Preparation Time: 10 minutes**

**Cooking Time: 25 minutes**

**Servings: 6**

**Ingredients:**

- 4 cups roasted chicken, shredded (Lunch Recipes: Roasted Lemon Chicken Sandwich)
- 2 tablespoons. butter
- 2 celery stalks, chopped
- 1 cup mushrooms, sliced
- 4 cups green cabbage, sliced into strips
- 2 garlic cloves, minced
- 6 cups chicken broth
- 1 carrot, sliced
- Salt and pepper to taste
- 1 tablespoon. garlic powder
- 1 tablespoon. onion powder

**Directions**:

1. Sauté the celery, mushrooms and garlic in the butter in a pot over medium heat for 4 minutes.
2. Add broth, carrots, garlic powder, onion powder, salt, and pepper.
3. Simmer for 10 minutes or until the vegetables are tender.
4. Add the chicken and cabbage and simmer for another 10 minutes or until the cabbage is tender.
5. Serve warm.
6. Can be refrigerated for up to 3 days or frozen for up to 1 month.

**Nutrition:**

Calories: 279 kcal          Protein: 33.4 g.

Carbs: 7.5 g

Fat: 12.3 g

## Chicken Avocado Salad

**Preparation Time: 7 minutes**

**Cooking Time: 10 minutes**

**Servings: 4**

**Ingredients:**

- 1 cup roasted chicken, shredded (Lunch Recipes: Roasted Lemon Chicken Sandwich)

- 1 bacon strip, cooked and chopped

- 1/2 medium avocado, chopped
- ¼ cup cheddar cheese, grated
- 1 hard-boiled egg, chopped
- 1 cup romaine lettuce, chopped
- 1 tablespoon. olive oil
- 1 tablespoon. apple cider vinegar
- Salt and pepper to taste

**Directions:**

1. Create the dressing by mixing apple cider vinegar, oil, salt and pepper.
2. Combine all the other ingredients in a mixing bowl.
3. Drizzle with the dressing and toss.
4. Can be refrigerated for up to 3 days.

**Nutrition:**

Calories: 220 kcal                    Protein: 14.8 g.

Carbs: 2.8 g

Fat: 16.7 g

# Chicken Broccoli Dinner

**Preparation Time: 10 minutes**

**Cooking Time: 5 minutes**

**Servings: 1**

**Ingredients:**

- 1 roasted chicken leg (Lunch Recipes: Roasted Lemon Chicken Sandwich)
- ½ cup broccoli florets
- ½ tablespoon. unsalted butter, softened
- 2 garlic cloves, minced
- Salt and pepper to taste

**Directions**:

1. Boil the broccoli in lightly salted water for 5 minutes. Drain the water from the pot and keep the broccoli in the pot. Keep the lid on to keep the broccoli warm.
2. Mix all the butter, garlic, salt and pepper in a small bowl to create garlic butter.
3. Place the chicken, broccoli and garlic butter.

**Nutrition:**

Calories: 257 kcal

Carbs: 5.1 g

Fat: 14 g

Protein: 27.4 g.

**Easy Meatballs**

**Preparation Time: 10 minutes**

**Cooking Time: 20 minutes**

 **Servings: 4**

**Ingredients:**

- 1 lb. ground beef
- 1 egg, beaten
- Salt and pepper to taste
- 1 teaspoon garlic powder
- 1 teaspoon onion powder
- 2 tablespoons. butter
- ¼ cup mayonnaise
- ¼ cup pickled jalapeños
- 1 cup cheddar cheese, grated

**Directions**

1. Combine the cheese, mayonnaise, pickled jalapenos, salt, pepper, garlic powder and onion powder in a large mixing bowl.
2. Add the beef and egg and combine using clean hands.
3. Form large meatballs. Makes about 12.
4. Fry the meatballs in the butter over medium heat for about 4 minutes on each side or until golden brown.
5. Serve warm with a keto-friendly side.
6. The meatball mixture can also be used to make a meatloaf. Just preheat your oven to 400 degrees F, press the mixture into a loaf pan and bake for about 30 minutes or until the top is golden brown.
7. Can be refrigerated for up to 5 days or frozen for up to 3 months.

**Nutrition:**

Calories: 454 kcal                    Protein: 43.2 g.

Carbs: 5 g

Fat: 28.2 g

# Chicken Casserole

**Preparation Time: 10 minutes**

**Cooking Time: 40 minutes**

**Servings: 8**

**Ingredients:**

- 1 lb. boneless chicken breasts, cut into 1" cubes
- 2 tablespoons. butter
- 4 tablespoons. green pesto
- 1 cup heavy whipping cream
- ¼ cup green bell peppers, diced
- 1 cup feta cheese, diced
- 1 garlic clove, minced
- Salt and pepper to taste

**Directions**

1. Preheat your oven to 400 degrees F.
2. Season the chicken with salt and pepper then batch fry in the butter until golden brown.
3. Place the fried chicken pieces in a baking dish. Add the feta cheese, garlic and bell peppers.
4. Combine the pesto and heavy cream in a bowl. Pour on top of the chicken mixture and spread with a spatula.
5. Bake for 30 minutes or until the casserole is light brown around the edges.
6. Serve warm.
7. Can be refrigerated for up to 5 days and frozen for 2 weeks.

**Nutrition:**

Calories: 294 kcal

Carbs: 1.7 g

Fat: 22.7 g

Protein: 20.1 g.

## Lemon Baked Salmon

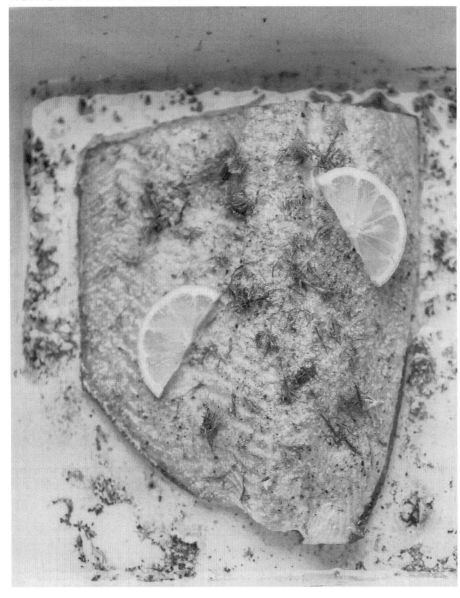

**Preparation Time: 10 minutes**

**Cooking Time: 30 minutes**

**Servings: 4**

**Ingredients:**

- 1 lb. salmon
- 1 tablespoon. olive oil
- Salt and pepper to taste
- 1 tablespoon. butter
- 1 lemon, thinly sliced
- 1 tablespoon. lemon juice

**Directions**:

1.  Preheat your oven to 400 degrees F.
2.  Grease a baking dish with the olive oil and place the salmon skin-side down.
3. Season the salmon with salt and pepper then top with the lemon slices.
4. Slice half the butter and place over the salmon.
5. Bake for 20minutes or until the salmon flakes easily.
6. Melt the remaining butter in a saucepan. When it starts to bubble, remove from heat and allow to cool before adding the lemon juice.
7. Drizzle the lemon butter over the salmon and Serve warm.

## Nutrition:

Calories: 211 kcal

Carbs: 1.5 g

Fat: 13.5 g

Protein: 22.2 g.

## Italian Sausage Stacks

**Preparation Time: 10 minutes**

**Cooking Time: 25 minutes**

**Servings: 3**

### Ingredients:

- 6 Italian sausage patties
- 4 tablespoon olive oil
- 2 ripe avocados, pitted
- 2 teaspoon fresh lime juice
- Salt and black pepper to taste
- 6 fresh eggs
- Red pepper flakes to garnish

### Directions:

1. In a skillet, warm the oil over medium heat and fry the sausage patties about 8 minutes until lightly browned and firm. Remove the patties to a plate.
2. Spoon the avocado into a bowl, mash with the lime juice, and season with salt and black pepper. Spread the mash on the sausages.
3. Boil 3 cups of water in a wide pan over high heat, and reduce to simmer (don't boil).
4. Crack each egg into a small bowl and gently put the egg into the simmering water; poach for 2 to 3 minutes. Use a perforated spoon to remove from the water on a paper towel to dry. Repeat with the other 5 eggs. Top each stack with a poached egg, sprinkle with chili flakes, salt, black pepper, and chives. Serve with turnip wedges.

### Nutrition:

Kcal 378,

Fat 23g,

Net Carbs 5g,

Protein 16g

## Baked Salmon
## Preparation Time: 10 minutes
## Cooking Time: 10 minutes
## Servings: 4
## Ingredients:

- Cooking spray
- 3 cloves garlic, minced
- ¼ cup butter
- 1 teaspoon lemon zest
- 2 tablespoons lemon juice
- 4 salmon fillets
- Salt and pepper to taste
- 2 tablespoons parsley, chopped

## Directions:

1. Preheat your oven to 425 degrees F.
2. Grease the pan with cooking spray.
3. In a bowl, mix the garlic, butter, and lemon zest and lemon juice.
4. Sprinkle salt and pepper on salmon fillets.
5. Drizzle with the lemon butter sauce.
6. Bake in the oven for 12 minutes.
7. Garnish with parsley before serving.

## Nutrition:

Calories 345

Total Fat 22.7g

Saturated Fat 8.9g

Cholesterol 109mg

Sodium 163mg

Total Carbohydrate 1.2g

Dietary Fiber 0.2g

Total Sugars 0.2g

Protein 34.9g

Potassium 718mg

**Tuna Patties**

**Preparation Time: 10 minutes**

**Cooking Time: 10 minutes**

**Servings: 8**

**Ingredients:**

- 20 oz. canned tuna flakes
- ¼ cup almond flour
- 1 egg, beaten
- 2 tablespoons fresh dill, chopped
- 2 stalks green onion, chopped
- Salt and pepper to taste
- 1 tablespoon lemon zest
- ¼ cup mayonnaise
- 1 tablespoon lemon juice
- 2 tablespoons avocado oil

**Directions:**

1. Combine all the ingredients except avocado oil, lemon juice and avocado oil in a large bowl.
2. Form 8 patties from the mixture.
3. In a pan over medium heat, add the oil.
4. Once the oil starts to sizzle, cook the tuna patties for 3 to 4 minutes per side.
5. Drain each patty on a paper towel.
6. Spread mayo on top and drizzle with lemon juice before serving.

## Nutrition:

Calories 101

Total Fat 4.9g

Saturated Fat 1.2g

Cholesterol 47mg

Sodium 243mg

Total Carbohydrate 3.1g

Dietary Fiber 0.5g

Total Sugars 0.7g

Protein 12.3g

Potassium 60mg

**Cauliflower Mash**

**Preparation Time: 10 minutes**

**Cooking Time: 5 minutes**

**Servings: 8**

**Ingredients:**

- 4 cups cauliflower florets, chopped
- 1 cup grated parmesan cheese
- 6 tablespoons. butter
- ½ lemon, juice and zest
- Salt and pepper to taste

**Directions**:

1. Boil the cauliflower in lightly salted water over high heat for 5 minutes or until the florets are tender but still firm.
2. Strain the cauliflower in a colander and add the cauliflower to a food processor
3. Add the remaining ingredients and pulse the mixture to a smooth and creamy consistency

4. Serve with protein like salmon, chicken or meatballs.
5. Can be refrigerated for up to 3 days.

**Nutrition:**

Calories: 101 kcal

Carbs: 3.1 g

Fat: 9.5 g

Protein: 2.2 g.

**Almond Waffles with Cinnamon Cream**

**Preparation Time: 10 minutes**

**Cooking Time: 25 minutes**

**Servings: 3**

**Ingredients:**

- For the Spread
- 8 oz. cream cheese, at room temperature
- 1 teaspoon cinnamon powder
- 3 tablespoon swerve brown sugar
- Cinnamon powder for garnishing
- For the Waffles
- 5 tablespoon melted butter
- 1 ½ cups unsweetened almond milk
- 7 large eggs
- ¼ teaspoon liquid stevia
- ½ teaspoon baking powder
- 1 ½ cups almond flour

## Directions:

1. Combine the cream cheese, cinnamon, and swerve with a hand mixer until smooth. Cover and chill until ready to use.
2. To make the waffles, whisk the butter, milk, and eggs in a medium bowl. Add the stevia and baking powder and mix. Stir in the almond flour and combine until no lumps exist. Let the batter sit for 5 minutes to thicken. Spritz a waffle iron with a non-stick cooking spray.
3. Ladle a ¼ cup of the batter into the waffle iron and cook according to the manufacturer's instructions until golden, about 10 minutes in total. Repeat with the remaining batter.
4. Slice the waffles into quarters; apply the cinnamon spread in between each of two waffles and snap. Sprinkle with cinnamon powder and serve.

## Nutrition:

Kcal 307,

Fat 24g,

Net Carbs 8g,

Protein 12g

## Grilled Mahi with Lemon Butter Sauce

**Preparation Time:** 20 minutes

**Cooking Time:** 10 minutes

**Servings:** 6

## Ingredients:

- 6 mahi fillets
- Salt and pepper to taste
- 2 tablespoons olive oil
- 6 tablespoons butter
- ¼ onion, minced
- ½ teaspoon garlic, minced
- ¼ cup chicken stock
- 1 tablespoon lemon juice

## Directions:

1. Preheat your grill to medium heat.
2. Season fish fillets with salt and pepper.
3. Coat both sides with olive oil.
4. Grill for 3 to 4 minutes per side.
5. Place fish on a serving platter.
6. In a pan over medium heat, add the butter and let it melt.
7. Add the onion and sauté for 2 minutes.
8. Add the garlic and cook for 30 seconds.
9. Pour in the chicken stock.
10. Simmer until the stock has been reduced to half.
11. Add the lemon juice.
12. Pour the sauce over the grilled fish fillets.

## Nutrition:

Calories 234

Total Fat 17.2g

Saturated Fat 8.3g

Cholesterol 117mg

Sodium 242mg

Total Carbohydrate 0.6g

Dietary Fiber 0.1g

Total Sugars 0.3g

Protein 19.1g

Potassium 385mg

# Dinner

**Beef-Stuffed Mushrooms**

**Preparation Time: 20 minutes**

**Cooking Time: 25 minutes**

**Servings: 4**

**Ingredients:**

- 4 mushrooms, stemmed
- 3 tablespoons olive oil, divided
- 1 yellow onion, sliced thinly
- 1 red bell pepper, sliced into strips
- 1 green bell pepper, sliced into strips
- Salt and pepper to taste
- 8 oz. beef, sliced thinly
- 3 oz. provolone cheese, sliced
- Chopped parsley

**Directions:**

1. Preheat your oven to 350 degrees F.
2. Arrange the mushrooms on a baking pan.
3. Brush with oil.
4. Add the remaining oil to a pan over medium heat.
5. Cook onion and bell peppers for 5 minutes.
6. Season with salt and pepper.
7. Place onion mixture on a plate.
8. Cook the beef in the pan for 5 minutes.
9. Sprinkle with salt and pepper.
10. Add the onion mixture back to the pan.
11. Mix well.
12. Fill the mushrooms with the beef mixture and cheese.
13. Bake in the oven for 15 minutes.

**Nutrition:**

Calories 333

Total Fat 20.3 g

Saturated Fat 6.7 g

Cholesterol 61 mg

Sodium 378 mg

Total Carbohydrate 8.2 g

Dietary Fiber 3.7 g

Protein 25.2 g

Total Sugars 7 g

Potassium 789 mg

## Rib Roast

## Preparation Time: 15 minutes

## Cooking Time: 3 hours

## Servings: 8

## Ingredients:

- 1 rib roast
- Salt to taste
- 12 cloves garlic, chopped
- 2 teaspoons lemon zest
- 6 tablespoons fresh rosemary, chopped
- 5 sprigs thyme

## Directions:

1. Preheat your oven to 325 degrees F.
2. Season all sides of rib roast with salt.
3. Place the rib roast in a baking pan.
4. Sprinkle with garlic, lemon zest and rosemary.
5. Add herb sprigs on top.
6. Roast for 3 hours.

Let rest for a few minutes and then slice and serve.

## Nutrition:

Calories 329

Total Fat 27 g

Saturated Fat 9 g

Cholesterol 59 mg

Sodium 498 mg

Total Carbohydrate 5.3 g

Dietary Fiber 1.8 g

Protein 18 g

Total Sugars 2 g

Potassium 493 mg

**Beef Stir Fry**

**Preparation Time: 15 minutes**

**Cooking Time: 10 minutes**

**Servings: 4**

**Ingredients:**

- 1 tablespoon soy sauce
- 1 tablespoon ginger, minced
- 1 teaspoon cornstarch
- 1 teaspoon dry sherry
- 12 oz. beef, sliced into strips
- 1 teaspoon toasted sesame oil
- 2 tablespoons oyster sauce
- 1 lb. baby bok choy, sliced
- 3 tablespoons chicken broth

**Directions:**

1. Mix soy sauce, ginger, cornstarch and dry sherry in a bowl.
2. Toss the beef in the mixture.
3. Pour oil into a pan over medium heat.
4. Cook the beef for 5 minutes, stirring.
5. Add oyster sauce, bok choy and chicken broth to the pan.
6. Cook for 1 minute.

## Nutrition:

Calories 247

Total Fat 15.8 g

Saturated Fat 4 g

Cholesterol 69 mg

Sodium 569 mg

Total Carbohydrate 6.3 g

Dietary Fiber 1.1 g

Protein 25 g


## Sweet & Sour Pork

**Preparation Time: 15 minutes**

**Cooking Time: 15 minutes**

**Servings: 4**

**Ingredients:**

- 1 lb. pork chops
- Salt and pepper to taste
- ½ cup sesame seeds
- 2 tablespoons peanut oil
- 2 tablespoons soy sauce
- 3 tablespoons apricot jam
- Chopped scallions

**Directions:**

1. Season pork chops with salt and pepper.
2. Press sesame seeds on both sides of pork.
3. Pour oil into a pan over medium heat.
4. Cook pork for 3 to 5 minutes per side.
5. Transfer to a plate.
6. In a bowl, mix soy sauce and apricot jam.

7. Simmer for 3 minutes.
8. Pour sauce over the pork and garnish with scallions before serving.

## Nutrition:

Calories 414

Total Fat 27.5 g

Saturated Fat 5.6 g

Cholesterol 68 mg

Sodium 607 mg

Total Carbohydrate 12.9 g

Dietary Fiber 1.8 g

Protein 29 g

Total Sugars 9 g

Potassium 332 mg

## Grilled Pork with Salsa

## Preparation Time: 30 minutes

## Cooking Time: 15 minutes

## Servings: 4

## Ingredients:

- Salsa
- 1 onion, chopped
- 1 tomato, chopped
- 1 peach, chopped
- 1 apricot, chopped
- 1 tablespoon olive oil
- 1 tablespoon lime juice
- 2 tablespoons fresh cilantro, chopped
- Salt and pepper to taste
- Pork
- 1 lb. pork tenderloin, sliced

- 1 tablespoon olive oil
- Salt and pepper to taste
- ½ teaspoon ground cumin
- ¾ teaspoon chili powder

## Directions:

1. Combine salsa ingredients in a bowl.
2. Cover and refrigerate.
3. Brush pork tenderloin with oil.
4. Season with salt, pepper, cumin and chili powder.
5. Grill pork for 5 to 7 minutes per side.
6. Slice pork and serve with salsa.

## Nutrition:

Calories 219

Total Fat 9.5 g

Saturated Fat 1.8 g

Cholesterol 74 mg

Sodium 512 mg

Total Carbohydrate 8.3 g

Dietary Fiber 1.5 g

Protein 24 g

Total Sugars 6 g

Potassium 600 mg

# Garlic Pork Loin

**Preparation Time: 15 minutes**

**Cooking Time: 1 hour**

**Servings: 6**

**Ingredients:**

- 1 ½ lb. pork loin roast
- 4 cloves garlic, sliced into slivers
- Salt and pepper to taste

**Directions:**

1. Preheat your oven to 425 degrees F.
2. Make several slits all over the pork roast.
3. Insert garlic slivers.
4. Sprinkle with salt and pepper.
5. Roast in the oven for 1 hour.

**Nutrition:**

Calories 235

Total Fat 13.3 g

Saturated Fat 2.6 g

Cholesterol 71 mg

Sodium 450 mg

Total Carbohydrate 1.7 g

Dietary Fiber 0.3 g

Protein 25.7 g

Total Sugars 3 g

Potassium 383 mg

**Chicken Pesto**

**Preparation Time: 15 minutes**

**Cooking Time: 25 minutes**

**Servings: 4**

**Ingredients:**

- 1 lb. chicken cutlet
- Salt and pepper to taste
- 1 tablespoon olive oil
- ½ cup onion, chopped
- ½ cup heavy cream
- ½ cup dry white wine
- 1 tomato, chopped
- ¼ cup pesto
- 2 tablespoons basil, chopped

**Directions:**

1. Season chicken with salt and pepper.
2. Pour oil into a pan over medium heat.
3. Cook chicken for 3 to 4 minutes per side.
4. Place the chicken on a plate.
5. Add the onion to the pan.
6. Cook for 1 minute.
7. Stir in the rest of the ingredients.
8. Bring to a boil.
9. Simmer for 15 minutes.
10. Put the chicken back to the pan.
11. Cook for 2 more minutes and then serve.

**Nutrition:**

Calories 371

Total Fat 23.7 g

Saturated Fat 9.2 g

Cholesterol 117 mg

Sodium 361 mg

Total Carbohydrate 5.7 g

Dietary Fiber 1 g

Protein 27.7 g

Total Sugars 3 g

Potassium 567 mg

## Garlic Parmesan Chicken Wings
**Preparation Time: 20 minutes**

**Cooking Time: 20 minutes**

**Servings: 8**

**Ingredients:**

- Cooking spray
- ½ cup all-purpose flour
- Pepper to taste
- 2 tablespoons garlic powder
- 3 eggs, beaten
- 1 ¼ cups Parmesan cheese, grated
- 2 cups breadcrumbs
- 2 lb. chicken wings

**Directions:**

1. Preheat your oven to 450 degrees F.
2. Spray baking pan with oil.
3. In a bowl, mix the flour, pepper and garlic powder.
4. Add eggs to another bowl.
5. Mix the Parmesan cheese and breadcrumbs in another bowl.
6. Dip the chicken wings in the first, second and third bowls.
7. Spray chicken wings with oil.
8. Bake in the oven for 20 minutes.

## Nutrition:

Calories 221

Total Fat 11.6 g

Saturated Fat 3.9 g

Cholesterol 122 mg

Sodium 242 mg

Total Carbohydrate 8 g

Dietary Fiber 0.4 g

Protein 16 g

Total Sugars 3 g

Potassium 163 mg

## Crispy Baked Shrimp
## Preparation Time: 15 minutes
## Cooking Time: 10 minutes
## Servings: 4
## Ingredients:

- ¼ cup whole-wheat breadcrumbs
- 3 tablespoons olive oil, divided
- 1 ½ lb. jumbo shrimp, peeled and deveined
- Salt and pepper to taste
- 2 tablespoons lemon juice
- 1 tablespoon garlic, chopped
- 2 tablespoons butter
- ¼ cup Parmesan cheese, grated
- 2 tablespoons chives, chopped

## Directions:

1. Preheat your oven to 425 degrees F.
2. Add breadcrumbs to a pan over medium heat.
3. Cook until toasted.

4. Transfer to a plate.
5. Coat baking pan with 1 tablespoon oil.
6. Arrange shrimp in a single layer in a baking pan.
7. Season with salt and pepper.
8. Mix lemon juice, garlic and butter in a bowl.
9. Pour mixture on top of the shrimp.
10. Add Parmesan cheese and chives to the breadcrumbs.
11. Sprinkle breadcrumbs on top of the shrimp.
12. Bake for 10 minutes.

## Nutrition:

Calories 340

Total Fat 18.7 g

Saturated Fat 6 g

Cholesterol 293 mg

Sodium 374 mg

Total Carbohydrate 6 g

Dietary Fiber 0.8 g

Protein 36.9 g

Total Sugars 2 g

Potassium 483 mg

## Herbed Mediterranean Fish Fillet

## Preparation Time: 20 minutes

## Cooking Time: 1 hour

## Servings: 6

## Ingredients:

- 3 lb. sea bass fillet
- Salt to taste
- 2 tablespoons tarragon, chopped
- ¼ cup dry white wine

- 3 tablespoons olive oil, divided
- 1 tablespoon butter
- 2 cloves garlic, minced
- 2 cups whole-wheat breadcrumbs
- 3 tablespoons parsley, chopped
- 3 tablespoons oregano, chopped
- 3 tablespoons fresh basil, chopped

## Directions:

1. Preheat your oven to 350 degrees F.
2. Season fish with salt and tarragon.
3. Pour half of oil into a roasting pan.
4. Stir in wine.
5. Add the fish in the roasting pan.
6. Bake in the oven for 50 minutes.
7. Add remaining oil to a pan over medium heat.
8. Cook herbs, breadcrumbs and salt.
9. Spread breadcrumb mixture on top of fish and bake for 5 minutes.

## Nutrition:

Calories 288

Total Fat 12.7 g

Saturated Fat 2.9 g

Cholesterol 65 mg

Sodium 499 mg

Total Carbohydrate 10.4 g

Dietary Fiber 1.8 g

Protein 29.5 g

Total Sugars 1 g

Potassium 401 mg

## Mushroom Stuffed with Ricotta

**Preparation Time: 10 minutes**

**Cooking Time: 10 minutes**

**Servings: 4**

**Ingredients:**

- 4 large mushrooms, stemmed
- 1 tablespoon olive oil
- Salt and pepper to taste
- ¼ cup basil, chopped
- 1 cup ricotta cheese
- ¼ cup Parmesan cheese, grated

**Directions:**

1. Preheat your grill.
2. Coat the mushrooms with oil.
3. Season with salt and pepper.
4. Grill for 5 minutes.
5. Stuff each mushroom with a mixture of basil, ricotta cheese and Parmesan cheese.
6. Grill for another 5 minutes.

**Nutrition:**

Calories 259

Total Fat 17.3 g

Saturated Fat 5.4 g

Cholesterol 24 mg

Sodium 509 mg

Total Carbohydrate 14.9 g

Dietary Fiber 2.6 g

Protein 12.2 g

Total Sugars 7 g

Potassium 572 mg

**Thai Chopped Salad**

**Preparation Time: 15 minutes**

**Cooking Time: 0 minutes**

**Servings: 4**

**Ingredients:**

- 10 oz. kale and cabbage mix
- 14 oz. tofu, sliced into cubes and fried crispy
- ½ cup vinaigrette

**Directions:**

1. Arrange kale and cabbage in a serving platter.
2. Top with the tofu cubes.
3. Drizzle with the vinaigrette.

**Nutrition:**

Calories 332

Total Fat 15 g

Saturated Fat 1.5 g

Cholesterol 0 mg

Sodium 236 mg

Total Carbohydrate 26.3 g

Dietary Fiber 7.6 g

Protein 1.3 g

Total Sugars 13 g

Potassium 41 mg

**Lemon & Rosemary Salmon**

**Preparation Time: 10 minutes**

**Cooking Time: 15 minutes**

**Servings: 4**

**Ingredients:**

- 4 salmon fillets
- Salt and pepper to taste
- 4 tablespoons butter
- 1 lemon, sliced
- 8 rosemary sprigs

**Directions:**

1. Season salmon with salt and pepper.
2. Place salmon on a foil sheet.
3. Top with butter, lemon slices and rosemary sprigs.
4. Fold the foil and seal.
5. Bake in the oven at 450 degrees F for 15 minutes.

**Nutrition:**

Calories 365

Total Fat 22 g

Saturated Fat 6 g

Cholesterol 86 mg

Sodium 445 mg

Total Carbohydrate 5 g

Dietary Fiber 1.9 g

Protein 29.8 g

Total Sugars 3 g

Potassium 782 mg

# Chicken Kurma

**Preparation Time: 20 minutes**

**Cooking Time: 25 minutes**

**Servings: 6**

**Ingredients:**

- 1 tablespoon olive oil
- 1 onion, diced
- 3 cloves garlic, sliced thinly
- 1 ginger, minced
- 2 tomatoes, diced
- 1 serrano pepper, minced
- Salt and pepper to taste
- 1 teaspoon ground turmeric
- 1 tablespoon tomato paste
- 1 ½ lb. chicken, sliced
- 1 red bell pepper, chopped

**Directions:**

1. Pour oil into a pan over medium heat.
2. Cook onion for 3 minutes.
3. Add garlic, ginger, tomatoes, Serrano pepper, salt, pepper, and turmeric and tomato paste.
4. Bring to a boil.
5. Reduce heat and simmer for 10 minutes.
6. Add chicken and cook for 5 minutes.
7. Stir in red bell pepper.
8. Cook for 5 minutes.

**Nutrition:**

Calories 175

Total Fat 15.2 g

Saturated Fat 3 g

Cholesterol 115 mg

Sodium 400 mg

Total Carbohydrate 7 g

Dietary Fiber 1.8 g

Protein 24 g

Total Sugars 3 g

Potassium 436 mg

## Pork Chops with Bacon & Mushrooms

## Preparation Time: 10 minutes

## Cooking Time: 20 minutes

## Servings: 4

## Ingredients:

- 6 strips bacon, chopped
- 4 pork chops
- Salt and pepper to taste
- 2 cloves garlic, minced
- 8 oz. mushrooms, sliced
- 1 tablespoon olive oil
- 5 sprigs fresh thyme
- 2/3 cup chicken broth
- 1/2 cup heavy cream

## Directions:

1. Cook bacon in a pan until crispy.
2. Transfer bacon on a plate.
3. Sprinkle salt and pepper on the pork chops.
4. Cook the pork chops in bacon fat for 4 minutes per side.
5. Transfer pork chops on a plate.
6. Add the garlic and mushrooms in the pan.
7. Add the olive oil
8. Cook for 5 minutes.
9. Pour in the broth and let the mixture boil.
10. Stir in the heavy cream and reduce the heat to low.

11. Put the bacon and pork chops back to the pan.
12. Cook for 3 more minutes before serving.

## Nutrition:

Calories 516

Total Fat 41.3g

Saturated Fat 15.4g

Cholesterol 121mg

Sodium 851mg

Total Carbohydrate 4.2g

Dietary Fiber 1.1g

Total Sugars 1.2g

Protein 31.7g

Potassium 679mg

## Pork

**Preparation Time: 10 minutes**

**Cooking Time: 20 minutes**

**Servings: 4**

## Ingredients:

- A single pound of pork tenderloin
- A quarter cup of oil
- 3 medium shallots (chop them finely)

## Directions:

1. Slice your pork into thick slices (go for about a half-inch thick).
2. Chop up your shallots before placing them on a plate.
3. Get a cast-iron skillet and warm up the oil

4. Press your pork into your shallots on both sides. Press firmly to make sure that they stick.
5. Place the slices of pork with shallots into the warm oil and then cook until it's done. The shallots may burn, but they will still be fine.
6. Make sure the pork is cooked through thoroughly.

**Nutrition:**

Calories-519

Fat-36 grams

Protein-46 grams

Carbs-7 grams

**Garlic Shrimp**

**Preparation Time: 10 minutes**

**Cooking Time: 30 minutes**

**Servings: 4**

**Ingredients:**

2 minced garlic cloves

2 whole garlic cloves

The juice from half a lemon

2 tablespoons of oil (olive)

2 tablespoons of butter

¾ pounds of either small or medium shrimp (it needs to be both shelled and deveined)

A quarter of a teaspoon of paprika

A quarter of a teaspoon of pepper flakes (red ones)

2 tablespoons of parsley that is chopped.

**Directions:**

Sprinkle your shrimp with a teaspoon of salt (fine grain sea salt) and let it sit for ten minutes.

Get a skillet.

Heat the butter with olive oil over a heat that is medium-high.

Add the flakes and garlic.

Sauté for half a minute.

Add your shrimp and cook until they have turned pink. This will take approximately two minutes. Stir constantly.

Add paprika and juice from the lemon.

Cook for another sixty seconds.

**Nutrition**

Per serving

Calories-260

Fat-18 grams

Carbs-none

Protein-24 protein

**Pork Chop**

**Preparation Time:** 10 minutes

**Cooking Time:** 30 minutes

**Servings:** 2

**Ingredients**:

- A dozen pork chop (boneless and thin cut)
- 2 cups of spinach (you should use baby spinach for this)
- 4 cloves of garlic
- A dozen slices provolone cheese

**Directions:**

1. Preheat your oven to a temperature of 350.

2. Press the garlic cloves using a garlic press. The cloves should go through the press and into a small bowl.
3. Spread the garlic that you have made onto one side of the pork chops.
4. Flip half a dozen chops while making sure the garlic side is down.
5. You should do this on a baking sheet that is rimmed.
6. Divide your spinach between the half dozen chops.
7. Fold cheese slices in half.
8. Put them on top of the spinach.
9. Put a second pork chop on top of the first set, but this time make sure that the garlic side is up.
10. Bake for 20 minutes.
11. Cover each chop with another piece of cheese.
12. Bake another 15 minutes.
13. Your meat meter should be at 160 degrees when you check with a thermometer.

## Nutrition:

Calories-436

Fat-25 grams

Carbs-2 grams

Protein-47 grams

## Citrus Egg Salad
## Preparation Time: 10 minutes

## Cooking Time: 20 minutes

## Servings: 3

## Ingredients:

- Half a dozen eggs (6)
- A single teaspoon of mustard (go with Dijon)
- 2 tablespoons of mayo
- A single teaspoon of lemon juice

## Directions:

1. Place the eggs gently in a medium saucepan.

2. Add cold water until your eggs are covered by an inch.
3. Bring to a boil.
4. You should do this for ten minutes. Remove from your heat and cool. Peel your eggs under running water that is cold.
5. Put your eggs in a food processor. Pulse until they are chopped.
6. Stir in condiments and juice.

## Nutrition:

Calories-222

Fat-19 grams

Protein-13 grams

Carbs-1 gram

## Chowder

**Preparation Time: 10 minutes**

**Cooking Time: 30 minutes**

**Servings: 4**

### Ingredients:

- A single tablespoon of butter
- 5 minced garlic cloves
- An entire head of cauliflower (cut it into florets that are small)
- Half of a teaspoon of oregano (use dried)
- Half a cup of carrots that have been diced
- Half a cup of onions that have been diced
- A cup and a half of broth (use vegetable)
- A quarter cup of cream cheese

### Directions:

1. Get a soup pot.
2. Heat your butter.
3. Add garlic and onions.
4. Sauté for a few moments.
5. Add the rest of the ingredients to the pot.

6. Bring to a boil.
7. Slow the heat and put it on a simmer.
8. Cook for 15 minutes.
9. Shut off the flame.
10. Use a hand blender to blend the soup partly in the pot.
11. Switch the flame back on.
12. Add a cup of broth.
13. Add the cream cheese.
14. Simmer for 10 minutes and switch off the flame again.

## Nutrition:

Calories-143

Fat-8.4 grams

Carbs-15.2 grams

Protein-4.5 grams

**Bulgur Appetizer Salad**

**Preparation Time: 30 minutes**

**Cooking Time: 0 minutes**

**Servings: 4**

**Ingredients:**

- 1 cup bulgur
- 2 cups hot water
- Black pepper to the taste
- 2 cups corn
- 1 cucumber, chopped
- 2 tablespoons lemon juice
- 2 tablespoons balsamic vinegar
- ¼ cup olive oil

**Directions**:

1. In a bowl, mix bulgur with the water, cover, leave aside for 30 minutes, fluff with a fork and transfer to a salad bowl.
2. Add corn, cucumber, oil with lemon juice, vinegar and pepper, toss, divide into small cups and serve.

**Nutrition:**

Calories 130

Fat 2

Fiber 2

Carbs 7

Protein 6

**Cocoa Bars**

**Preparation Time: 2 hours**

**Cooking Time: 0 minutes**

**Servings: 12**

**Ingredients:**

- 1 cup unsweetened cocoa chips
- 2 cups rolled oats
- 1 cup low-fat peanut butter
- ½ cup chia seeds
- ½ cup raisins
- ¼ cup coconut sugar
- ½ cup coconut milk

**Directions**:

1. Put 1 and ½ cups oats in your blender, pulse well, transfer this to a bowl, add the rest of the oats, cocoa chips, chia seeds, raisins, sugar and milk, stir really well, spread this into a square pan, press well, keep in the fridge for 2 hours, slice into 12 bars and serve.

## Nutrition:

Calories 198

Fat 5

Fiber 4

Carbs 10

Protein 89

## Cinnamon Apple Chips

**Preparation Time: 10 minutes**

**Cooking Time: 2 hours**

**Servings: 4**

**Ingredients:**

- Cooking spray
- 2 teaspoons cinnamon powder
- 2 apples, cored and thinly sliced

## Directions:

1. Arrange apple slices on a lined baking sheet, spray them with cooking oil, sprinkle cinnamon, introduce in the oven and bake at 300 degrees F for 2 hours.
2. Divide into bowls and serve as a snack.

## Nutrition:

Calories 80

Fat 0

Fiber 3

Carbs 7

Protein 4

**Greek Party Dip**

**Preparation Time: 10 minutes**

**Cooking Time: 0 minutes**

**Servings: 4**

**Ingredients:**

- ½ cup coconut cream
- 1 cup fat-free Greek yogurt
- 2 teaspoons dill, dried
- 2 teaspoons thyme, dried
- 1 teaspoon sweet paprika
- 2 teaspoons no-salt-added sun-dried tomatoes, chopped
- 2 teaspoons parsley, chopped
- 2 teaspoons chives, chopped
- Black pepper to the taste

**Directions:**

1. In a bowl, mix cream with yogurt, dill with thyme, paprika, tomatoes, parsley, chives and pepper, stir well, divide into smaller bowls and serve as a dip.

**Nutrition:**

Calories 100

Fat 1

Fiber 4

Carbs 8

Protein 3

**Spicy Pumpkin Seeds Bowls**

**Preparation Time: 10 minutes**

**Cooking Time: 20 minutes**

**Servings: 6**

**Ingredients:**

- ½ tablespoon chili powder
- ½ teaspoon cayenne pepper
- 2 cups pumpkin seeds
- 2 teaspoons lime juice

**Directions:**

1. Spread pumpkin seeds on a lined baking sheet, add lime juice, cayenne and chili powder, toss well, introduce in the oven, roast at 275 degrees F for 20 minutes, divide into small bowls and serve as a snack.

**Nutrition:**

Calories 170

Fat 2

Fiber 7

Carbs 12

Protein 6

**Apple and Pecans Bowls**

**Preparation Time: 10 minutes**

**Cooking Time: 0 minutes**

**Servings: 4**

**Ingredients:**

- 4 big apples, cored, peeled and cubed
- 2 teaspoons lemon juice
- ¼ cup pecans, chopped

**Directions:**

1. In a bowl, mix apples with lemon juice and pecans, toss, divide into small bowls and serve as a snack.

**Nutrition:**

Calories 120

Fat 4

Fiber 3

Carbs 12

Protein 3

**Shrimp Muffins**

**Preparation Time: 10 minutes**

**Cooking Time: 45 minutes**

**Servings: 6**

**Ingredients:**

- 1 spaghetti squash, peeled and halved
- 2 tablespoons avocado mayonnaise
- 1 cup low-fat mozzarella cheese, shredded
- 8 ounces' shrimp, peeled, cooked and chopped

- 1 and ½ cups almond flour
- 1 teaspoon parsley, dried
- 1 garlic clove, minced
- Black pepper to the taste
- Cooking spray

**Directions**:

1. Arrange the squash on a lined baking sheet, introduce in the oven at 375 degrees F, bake for 30 minutes, scrape flesh into a bowl, add pepper, parsley flakes, flour, shrimp, mayo and mozzarella and stir well, divide this mix into a muffin tray greased with cooking spray, bake in the oven at 375 degrees F for 15 minutes and serve them cold as a snack.

**Nutrition:**

Calories 140

Fat 2

Fiber 4

Carbs 14

Protein 12

**Zucchini Bowls**

**Preparation Time: 10 minutes**

**Cooking Time: 20 minutes**

**Servings: 12**

**Ingredients:**

- Cooking spray
- ½ cup dill, chopped
- 1 egg
- ½ cup whole wheat flour
- Black pepper to the taste
- 1 yellow onion, chopped
- 2 garlic cloves, minced

- 3 zucchinis, grated

**Directions**:

1. In a bowl, mix zucchinis with garlic, onion, flour, pepper, egg and dill, stir well, shape small bowls out of this mix, arrange them on a lined baking sheet, grease them with some cooking spray, bake at 400 degrees F for 20 minutes, flipping them halfway, divide them into bowls and serve as a snack.

**Nutrition:**

Calories 120,

Fat 1

Fiber 4

Carbs 12

Protein 6

**Cheesy Mushrooms Caps**

**Preparation Time: 10 minutes**

**Cooking Time: 30 minutes**

**Servings: 20**

**Ingredients:**

- 20 white mushroom caps
- 1 garlic clove, minced
- 3 tablespoons parsley, chopped
- 2 yellow onions, chopped
- Black pepper to the taste
- ½ cup low-fat parmesan, grated
- ¼ cup low-fat mozzarella, grated
- A drizzle of olive oil
- 2 tablespoons non-fat yogurt

**Directions**:

1. Heat up a pan with some oil over medium heat, add garlic and onion, stir, cook for 10 minutes and transfer to a bowl.
2. Add black pepper, garlic, parsley, mozzarella, parmesan and yogurt, stir well, stuff the mushroom caps with this mix, arrange them on a lined baking sheet, bake in the oven at 400 degrees F for 20 minutes and serve them as an appetizer.

**Nutrition:**

Calories 120,

Fat 1

Fiber 3

Carbs 11

Protein 7

## Mozzarella Cauliflower Bars

Jim Westphalen

**Preparation Time: 10 minutes**

**Cooking Time: 40 minutes**

**Servings: 12**

**Ingredients:**

- 1 big cauliflower head, riced
- ½ cup low-fat mozzarella cheese, shredded
- ¼ cup egg whites
- 1 teaspoon Italian seasoning
- Black pepper to the taste

**Directions:**

1. Spread the cauliflower rice on a lined baking sheet, cook in the oven at 375 degrees F for 20 minutes, transfer to a bowl, add black pepper, cheese, seasoning and egg whites, stir well, spread into a rectangle pan and press well on the bottom.
2. Introduce in the oven at 375 degrees F, bake for 20 minutes, cut into 12 bars and serve as a snack.

**Nutrition:**

Calories 140                    Protein 6

Fat 1

Fiber 3

Carbs 6

**Shrimp and Pineapple Salsa**

**Preparation Time: 10 minutes**

**Cooking Time: 40 minutes**

**Servings: 4**

**Ingredients:**

- 1-pound large shrimp, peeled and deveined
- 20 ounces canned pineapple chunks
- 1 tablespoon garlic powder
- 1 cup red bell peppers, chopped
- Black pepper to the taste

**Directions**:

1. Place shrimp in a baking dish, add pineapple, garlic, bell peppers and black pepper, toss a bit, introduce in the oven, bake at 375 degrees F for 40 minutes, divide into small bowls and serve cold.

**Nutrition:**

Calories 170

Fat 5

Fiber 4

Carbs 15

Protein 11

**Strawberry Buckwheat Pancakes**

**Preparation Time: 20 minutes**

**Cooking Time: 5 minutes**

**Servings: 4**

**Ingredients:**

- 100g (3½oz) strawberries, chopped
- 100g (3½ oz.) buckwheat flour
- 1 egg
- 250mls (8fl oz.) milk
- 1 teaspoon olive oil
- 1 teaspoon olive oil for frying
- Freshly squeezed juice of 1 orange
- 175 calories per serving

**Directions**:

1. Pour the milk into a bowl and mix in the egg and a teaspoon of olive oil. Sift in the flour to the liquid mixture until smooth and creamy. Allow it to rest for 15 minutes. Heat a little oil in a pan and pour in a quarter of the mixture (or to the size you prefer.) Sprinkle in a quarter of the strawberries into the batter. Cook for around 2 minutes on each side. Serve hot with a drizzle of orange juice. You could try experimenting with other berries such as blueberries and blackberries

**Nutrition:**

Calories

Fat

Fiber

Carbs

Protein

**Strawberry & Nut Granola**

**Preparation Time: 10 minutes**

**Cooking Time: 50 minutes**

**Servings: 12**

**Ingredients:**

- 200g (7oz) oats
- 250g (9oz) buckwheat flakes
- 100g (3½ oz.) walnuts, chopped
- 100g (3½ oz.) almonds, chopped
- 100g (3½ oz.) dried strawberries
- 1½ teaspoons ground ginger
- 1½ teaspoons ground cinnamon
- 120mls (4fl oz.) olive oil
- 2 tablespoon honey

**Directions:**

1. Combine the oats, buckwheat flakes, nuts, ginger and cinnamon. In a saucepan, warm the oil and honey. Stir until the honey has melted. Pour the warm oil into the dry ingredients and mix well. Spread the mixture out on a large baking tray (or two) and bake in the oven at 150C (300F) for around 50 minutes until the granola is golden. Allow it to cool. Add in the dried berries. Store in an airtight container until ready to use. Can be served with yogurt, milk or even dry as a handy snack.

**Nutrition:**

Calories 391

Fat 0

Fiber 6

Carbs 3

Protein 8

# Chilled Strawberry & Walnut Porridge

**Preparation Time: 10 minutes**

**Cooking Time: 0 minutes**

**Servings: 1**

**Ingredients:**

- 100g (3½ oz.) strawberries
- 50g (2oz) rolled oats
- 4 walnut halves, chopped
- 1 teaspoon chia seeds
- 200mls (7fl oz.) unsweetened soya milk
- 100ml (3½ FL oz.) water

**Directions:**

1. Place the strawberries, oats, soya milk and water into a blender and process until smooth. Stir in the chia seeds and mix well. Chill in the fridge overnight and serve in the morning with a sprinkling of chopped walnuts. It's simple and delicious.

**Nutrition:**

Calories 384

Fat 2

Fiber 5

Carbs 3

Protein7

# Fruit & Nut Yogurt Crunch

**Preparation Time: 5 minutes**

**Cooking Time: 0 minutes**

**Servings: 1**

**Ingredients:**

- 100g (3½ oz.) plain Greek yogurt
- 50g (2oz) strawberries, chopped
- 6 walnut halves, chopped
- Sprinkling of cocoa powder

**Directions:**

1. Stir half of the chopped strawberries into the yogurt. Using a glass, place a layer of yogurt with a sprinkling of strawberries and walnuts, followed by another layer of the same until you reach the top of the glass. Garnish with walnuts pieces and a dusting of cocoa powder.

## Nutrition:

Calories 296

Protein 9

Fat 4

Fiber 2

Carbs 5

**Cheesy Baked Eggs**

**Preparation Time: 5 minutes**

**Cooking Time: 15 minutes**

**Servings: 4**

**Ingredients:**

- 4 large eggs
- 75g (3oz) cheese, grated
- 25g (1oz) fresh rocket (arugula) leaves, finely chopped
- 1 tablespoon parsley
- ½ teaspoon ground turmeric
- 1 tablespoon olive oil

**Directions**:

1. Grease each ramekin dish with a little olive oil. Divide the rocket (arugula) between the ramekin dishes then break an egg into each one. Sprinkle a little parsley and turmeric on top then sprinkle on the cheese. Place the ramekins in a preheated oven at 220C/425F for 15 minutes, until the eggs are set and the cheese is bubbling.

**Nutrition:**

Calories 198

Fat 9

Fiber 3

Carbs 2

Protein 13

**Green Egg Scramble**

**Preparation Time: 10 minutes**

**Cooking Time: 5 minutes**

**Servings: 1**

**Ingredients**:

- 2 eggs, whisked
- 25g (1oz) rocket (arugula) leaves
- 1 teaspoon chives, chopped
- 1 teaspoon fresh basil, chopped
- 1 teaspoon fresh parsley, chopped
- 1 tablespoon olive oil

**Directions**:

1. Mix the eggs together with the rocket (arugula) and herbs. Heat the oil in a frying pan and pour into the egg mixture. Gently stir until it's lightly scrambled. Season and serve.

**Nutrition:**

Calories 250

Fat 5

Fiber 7

Carbs 8

Protein 11

**Spiced Scramble**

**Preparation Time: 10 minutes**

**Cooking Time: 5 minutes**

**Servings: 1**

**Ingredients:**

- 25g (1oz) kale, finely chopped
- 2 eggs
- 1 spring onion (scallion) finely chopped
- 1 teaspoon turmeric
- 1 tablespoon olive oil
- Sea salt
- Freshly ground black pepper

**Directions**:

1. Crack the eggs into a bowl. Add the turmeric and whisk them. Season with salt and pepper. Heat the oil in a frying pan, add the kale and spring onions (scallions) and cook until it has wilted. Pour in the beaten eggs and stir until eggs have scrambled together with the kale.

**Nutrition:**

Calories 259

Fat 3

Fiber 4

Carbs 3

Protein 9

## Potato Bites

**Preparation Time: 10 minutes**

**Cooking Time: 20 minutes**

**Servings: 3**

**Ingredients:**

- 1 potato, sliced
- 2 bacon slices, already cooked and crumbled
- 1 small avocado, pitted and cubed
- Cooking spray

**Directions**:

1. Spread potato slices on a lined baking sheet, spray with cooking oil, introduce in the oven at 350 degrees F, bake for 20 minutes, arrange on a platter, top each slice with avocado and crumbled bacon and serve as a snack.

**Nutrition:**

Calories 180

Fat 4

Fiber 1

Carbs 8

Protein 6

## Eggplant Salsa

**Preparation Time: 10 minutes**

**Cooking Time: 10 minutes**

**Servings: 4**

**Ingredients:**

- 1 and ½ cups tomatoes, chopped
- 3 cups eggplant, cubed
- A drizzle of olive oil
- 2 teaspoons capers

- 6 ounces' green olives, pitted and sliced
- 4 garlic cloves, minced
- 2 teaspoons balsamic vinegar
- 1 tablespoon basil, chopped
- Black pepper to the taste

**Directions**:

1. Heat a saucepan with the oil medium-high heat, add eggplant, stir and cook for 5 minutes.
2. Add tomatoes, capers, olives, garlic, vinegar, basil and black pepper, toss, cook for 5 minutes more, divide into small cups and serve cold.

**Nutrition:**

Calories 120

Fat 6

Fiber 5

Carbs 9

Protein 7

## Carrots and Cauliflower Spread

**Preparation Time: 10 minutes**

**Cooking Time: 40 minutes**

**Servings: 4**

**Ingredients:**

- 1 cup carrots, sliced
- 2 cups cauliflower florets
- ½ cup cashews
- 2 and ½ cups water
- 1 cup almond milk
- 1 teaspoon garlic powder
- ¼ teaspoon smoked paprika

**Directions**:

1. In a small pot, mix the carrots with cauliflower, cashews and water, stir, cover, bring to a boil over medium heat, cook for 40 minutes, drain and transfer to a blender.
2. Add almond milk, garlic powder and paprika, pulse well, divide into small bowls and serve

**Nutrition:**

Calories 201

Fat 7

Fiber 4

Carbs 7

Protein 7

**Black Bean Salsa**

**Preparation Time: 10 minutes**

**Cooking Time: 0 minutes**

**Servings: 6**

**Ingredients:**

- 1 tablespoon coconut aminos
- ½ teaspoon cumin, ground
- 1 cup canned black beans, no-salt-added, drained and rinsed
- 1 cup salsa
- 6 cups romaine lettuce leaves, torn
- ½ cup avocado, peeled, pitted and cubed

**Directions**:

1. In a bowl, combine the beans with the aminos, cumin, salsa, lettuce and avocado, toss, divide into small bowls and serve as a snack.

**Nutrition:**

Calories 181

Fat 4

Fiber 7

Carbs 14

Protein 7

**Mung Sprouts Salsa**

**Preparation Time: 10 minutes**

**Cooking Time: 0 minutes**

**Servings: 2**

**Ingredients:**

- 1 red onion, chopped
- 2 cups Mung beans, sprouted
- A pinch of red chili powder

- 1 green chili pepper, chopped
- 1 tomato, chopped
- 1 teaspoon chaat masala
- 1 teaspoon lemon juice
- 1 tablespoon coriander, chopped
- Black pepper to the taste

## Directions:

1. In a salad bowl, mix onion with Mung sprouts, chili pepper, tomato, chili powder, chaat masala, lemon juice, coriander and pepper, toss well, divide into small cups and serve.

## Nutrition:

Calories 100

Fiber 1

Fat 3

Carbs 3

Protein 6

## Sprouts and Apples Snack Salad

**Preparation Time: 10 minutes**

**Cooking Time: 0 minutes**

**Servings: 4**

## Ingredients:

- 1-pound Brussels sprouts, shredded
- 1 cup walnuts, chopped
- 1 apple, cored and cubed
- 1 red onion, chopped
- For the salad dressing:
- 3 tablespoons red vinegar
- 1 tablespoon mustard
- ½ cup olive oil
- 1 garlic clove, minced
- Black pepper to the taste

## Directions:

1. In a salad bowl, mix sprouts with apple, onion and walnuts.
2. In another bowl, mix vinegar with mustard, oil, garlic and pepper, whisk really well, add this to your salad, toss well and serve as a snack.

## Nutrition:

Calories 120

Fat 2

Fiber 2

Carbs 8

Protein 6

## Dijon Celery Salad

**Preparation Time: 10 minutes**

**Cooking Time: 0 minutes**

**Servings: 4**

## Ingredients:

- 5 teaspoons stevia
- ½ cup lemon juice
- 1/3 cup Dijon mustard
- 2/3 cup olive oil
- Black pepper to the taste
- 2 apples, cored, peeled and cubed
- 1 bunch celery and leaves, roughly chopped
- ¾ cup walnuts, chopped

## Directions:

1. In a salad bowl, mix celery and its leaves with apple pieces and walnuts.
2. Add black pepper, lemon juice, mustard, stevia and olive oil, whisk well, add to your salad, toss, divide into small cups and serve as a snack.

## Nutrition:

Calories 125

Fat 2

Fiber 2

Carbs 7

Protein 7

## Napa Cabbage Slaw

**Preparation Time: 10 minutes**
**Cooking Time: 0 minutes**

**Servings: 4**

**Ingredients:**

- ½ cup of red bell pepper, cut into thin strips
- 1 carrot, grated
- 4 cups Napa cabbage, shredded
- 3 green onions, chopped
- 1 tablespoon olive oil
- 2 teaspoons ginger, grated
- ½ teaspoon red pepper flakes, crushed
- 3 tablespoons balsamic vinegar
- 1 tablespoon coconut aminos
- 3 tablespoons low-fat peanut butter

**Directions**:

1. In a salad bowl, mix bell pepper with carrot, cabbage and onions and toss.
2. Add oil, ginger, pepper flakes, vinegar, aminos and peanut butter, toss, divide into small cups and serve.

## Nutrition:

Calories 160

Fat 10

Fiber 3

Carbs 10

Protein 5

## Dill Bell Pepper Bowls

**Preparation Time: 10 minutes**

**Cooking Time: 0 minutes**

**Servings: 4**

**Ingredients:**

- 2 tablespoons dill, chopped
- 1 yellow onion, chopped
- 1 pound multi colored bell peppers, cut into halves, seeded and cut into thin strips
- 3 tablespoons olive oil
- 2 and ½ tablespoons white vinegar
- Black pepper to the taste

**Directions**:

1. In a salad bowl, mix bell peppers with onion, dill, pepper, oil and vinegar, toss to coat, divide into small bowls and serve as a snack.

**Nutrition:**

Calories 120

Fat 3

Fiber 4

Carbs 2

Protein 3

## Baked Lemon & Pepper Chicken

**Preparation Time: 20 minutes**

**Cooking Time: 25 minutes**

**Servings: 4**

**Ingredients:**

- 4 chicken breast fillets
- Salt to taste
- 1 tablespoon olive oil
- 1 lemon, sliced thinly
- 1 tablespoon maple syrup
- 2 tablespoons lemon juice
- 2 tablespoons butter
- Pepper to taste

**Directions:**

1. Preheat your oven to 425 degrees F.
2. Season chicken with salt.
3. Pour oil into a pan over medium heat.
4. Cook chicken for 5 minutes per side.
5. Transfer chicken to a baking pan.
6. Surround the chicken with the lemon slices.
7. Bake in the oven for 10 minutes.
8. Pour in maple syrup and lemon juice to the pan.
9. Put the butter on top of the chicken.
10. Sprinkle with pepper.
11. Bake for another 5 minutes.

**Nutrition:**

Calories 286

Total Fat 13 g

Saturated Fat 5 g

Cholesterol 109 mg

Sodium 448 mg

Total Carbohydrate 7 g

Dietary Fiber 1.4 g

Protein 34.8 g

Total Sugars 3 g

Potassium 350 mg

# Vegetables

## Tomato and broccoli soup

**Preparation Time**: 50 minutes

**Cooking Time:** 55 minutes

**Servings**: 4

**Ingredients:**

- A drizzle of olive oil
- Canned sugar-free tomatoes- 28 oz.
- Crushed red pepper- ¼ tsp.
- Broccoli head: into florets- 1
- Small ginger: chopped- 1
- Onion: chopped – 1
- Garlic clove: minced- 1
- Coriander seeds- 2 tsp.
- Black pepper
- Salt

**Directions:**

1. Boil water and salt in a pan on medium-high and add broccoli florets to steam for 2 minutes.
2. Remove and put in a bowl of ice water. Drain and set aside.
3. Heat pan and put in coriander seeds to toast for 4 minutes. Blend in a blender and set aside.
4. Pour olive oil in a pot and set to medium and add red pepper, salt, pepper and onions and cook for 7 minutes.
5. Mix in coriander seeds and garlic and let it cook for 3 minutes.
6. Pour in tomatoes and let simmer for 10 minutes.
7. Mix in broccoli and cook for 12 minutes.
8. Serve

**Nutrition:**

Calories- 152, carbs- 1, protein- 9, fiber- 8, fats- 9

## Bok Choy Stir Fry with Fried Bacon Slices

**Preparation Time**: 17 minutes

**Cooking Time:** 15 minutes

**Servings**: 2

**Ingredients:**

- Bok choy; chopped - 2 cup.
- Garlic cloves; minced - 2
- Bacon slices; chopped - 2
- A drizzle of avocado oil
- Salt and black pepper to the taste.

**Instructions:**

1. Take a pan and heat it with oil over medium heat.
2. When the oil is hot, add bacon and keep stirring it until it's brown and crispy.
3. Transfer them to paper towels to drain out the excess oil.
4. Now bring the pan to medium heat and in it add garlic and bok choy.
5. Again give it a stir and cook it for 5 minutes.
6. Now drizzle and add some salt, pepper and the fried bacon and stir them for another 1 minute.
7. Turn off the heat and divide them in plates to serve.

### Nutrition

Calories: 50; Fat: 1; Fiber: 1; Carbs: 2; Protein: 2

## Broccoli-cauliflower stew

**Preparation Time**: 25 minutes

**Cooking Time:** 15 minutes

**Servings**: 5

**Ingredients:**

- Bacon slices: chopped -2
- Cauliflower head: separated into florets- 1
- Broccoli head: separated into florets- 1
- Butter- 2 tbsp.

- Garlic cloves: minced- 2
- Salt
- Black pepper

## Directions:

1. Put a pan on medium heat and dissolve the butter and the garlic. Add the bacon slices to brown for 3 minutes all over.
2. Mix in broccoli and cauliflower florets to cook for 2 minutes.
3. Pour water over it and cover the lid and let cook for 10 minutes.
4. Season with pepper and salt and puree soup with a dipping blend.
5. Let boil slowly for some minutes on medium heat.
6. Serve into bowls.

## Nutrition:

Calories- 128, carbs- 4, protein- 6, fiber- 7, fats- 2

## Creamy Avocado Soup

**Preparation Time**: 20 minutes

**Cooking Time:** 15 minutes

**Servings**: 4

## Ingredients:

- Chicken stock, 3 c.
- Black pepper
- Chopped scallions, 2
- Salt
- Heavy cream, 2/3 c.
- Butter, 2 tbsps.
- Chopped avocados, 2

## Directions:

1. Over a medium source of heat, set the saucepan and cook the scallions for 2 minutes
2. Stir in 2 ½ cups stock to simmer for 3 minutes
3. Set the blender in position to blend avocados, heavy cream, the remaining stock, and seasonings.

4. Return to a pan to cook for 2 minutes as you adjust the seasoning
5. Serve in soup bowls

**Nutrition:**

Calories: 335, Fat: 32, Fiber: 9, Carbs: 13, Protein: 3

## Bok choy mushroom soup

**Preparation Time**: 25 minutes

**Cooking Time:** 15 minutes

**Servings**: 4

**Ingredients:**

- Bacon strips: chopped- 2
- Beef stock- 3 cups
- Bok choy: chopped- 1 bunch
- Onion: chopped- 1
- Parmesan cheese: grated- 3 tbsp.
- Coconut aminos- 3 tbsp.
- Worcestershire sauce- 2 tbsp.
- Red pepper flakes- ½ tbsp.
- Mushrooms: chopped- 1½ cups
- Black Pepper
- Salt

**Directions:**

1. Put bacon in a saucepan over medium-high heat to brown until crispy then remove to paper towels to drain.
2. To medium heat, add the mushrooms and onions in the pan and cook for 15 minutes.
3. Pour in the stock, pepper flakes, aminos, bok choy, Worcestershire sauce, salt and pepper and mix.
4. Cook until bok choy is tender.
5. Serve into bowls and sprinkle with Parmesan cheese and bacon.

**Nutrition:**

Calories- 100, carbs- 1, protein- 5, fiber- 9, fats- 5

**Tasty Radish Soup**

**Preparation Time**: 30 minutes

**Cooking Time:** 45 minutes

**Servings**: 4

**Ingredients:**

- Chopped onion, 1
- Salt
- Chopped celery stalk, 2
- Chicken stock, 6 c.
- Coconut oil, 3 tbsps.
- Quartered radishes, 2 bunches
- Black pepper
- Minced garlic cloves, 6

**Directions:**

1. Set the pan over medium heat and melt the oil
2. Stir in the celery, onion, and garlic to cook until soft, about 5 minutes
3. Stir in the stock, radishes, and seasonings.
4. Cover and simmer to boil for 15 minutes
5. Enjoy while still hot

**Nutrition:**

Calories: 131, Fat: 12, Fiber: 8, Carbs: 4, Protein: 1

**Fried garlicy bacon and bok choy broth**

**Preparation Time**: 17 minutes

**Cooking Time:** 15 minutes

**Servings**: 2

**Ingredients:**

- Bok choy: chopped- 2 cups
- A drizzle of avocado oil
- Bacon slices: chopped- 2
- Garlic cloves: minced- 2
- Black pepper
- Salt

**Directions:**

1. Put bacon in a pan on medium heat and let crisp. Remove and let drain on paper towels.
2. Add bok choy and garlic to the pan and let cook for 4 minutes.
3. Season with pepper and salt and put the bacon back into the pan.
4. Let cook for 1 minute and serve.

**Nutrition:**

Calories- 116, carbs- 8, protein- 3, fiber- 8, fats- 1

**Nutritional Mustard Greens and Spinach Soup**

**Preparation Time**: 25 minutes

**Cooking Time:** 15 minutes

**Servings**: 6

**Ingredients:**

- Spinach; torn - 5 cups.
- Fenugreek seeds - 1/2 teaspoon.
- Cumin seeds - 1 teaspoon.
- Jalapeno; chopped - 1 tablespoon.
- Mustard greens; chopped - 5 cups.
- Ghee - 2 teaspoons.

- Paprika - 1/2 teaspoon.
- Avocado oil - 1 tablespoon.
- Coriander seeds - 1 teaspoon.
- Yellow onion; chopped - 1 cup.
- Garlic; minced - 1 tablespoon.
- Ginger; grated - 1 tablespoon.
- Turmeric; ground - 1/2 teaspoon.
- Coconut milk - 3 cups.
- Salt and black pepper to the taste.

**Directions:**

1. Add coriander, fenugreek and cumin seed in a heated pot with oil over medium high heat.
2. Now stir and brow them for 2 minutes.
3. In the same pot, add onions and again stir them for 3 minutes.
4. Now after the onion's cooked, add half of the garlic, jalapenos, ginger and turmeric.
5. Again, give it a good stir and cook for another 3 minutes.
6. Add some more mustard greens, spinach and saute everything for 10 minutes.
7. After it's done add milk, salt, pepper before blending the soup with an immersion blender.
8. Now take another pan and heat it up over medium heat with some ghee drizzled on it.
9. In it, add garlic, paprika, and give it a good stir before turning off the heat.
10. Bring the soup to heat over medium heat and transfer them into soup bowls.
11. Top it with some drizzles of ghee and paprika. Now it's ready to serve hot.

**Nutrition:**

Calories: - 143; Fat: 6; Fiber: 3; Carbs: 7; Protein: 7

**Hash Browns with Radish**

**Preparation Time**: 20 minutes

**Cooking Time:** 15 minutes

**Servings**: 4

**Ingredients:**

- Shredded Parmesan cheese, 1/3 c.
- Garlic powder, ½ tsp.
- Salt
- Shredded radishes, 1 lb.
- Black pepper
- Onion powder, ½ tsp.
- Medium eggs, 4

**Directions:**

1. Set a large mixing bowl in a working surface.
2. Combine the seasonings, radishes, eggs, onion, and parmesan cheese
3. Arrange the mixture in a well-lined baking tray.
4. Set the oven for 10 minutes at 3750F. Allow to bake
5. Enjoy while still hot

**Nutrition:**

Calories: 104, Fat: 6, Fiber: 8, Carbs: 5, Protein: 6

**Baked Radishes**

**Preparation Time**: 30 minutes

**Cooking Time:** 35 minutes

**Servings**: 4

**Ingredients:**

- Chopped chives, 1 tbsp.
- Sliced radishes, 15
- Salt
- Vegetable oil cooking spray
- Black pepper

## Directions:

1. Line your baking sheet well then spray with the cooking spray
2. Set the sliced radishes on the baking tray then sprinkle with cooking oil
3. Add the seasonings then top with chives
4. Set the oven for 10 minutes at 375oF, allow to bake
5. Turn the radishes to bake for 10 minutes
6. Serve cold

## Nutrition:

Calories: 63, Fat: 8, Fiber: 3, Carbs: 6, Protein: 1

## Coleslaw Avocado Salad

**Preparation Time**: 10 minutes

**Cooking Time:** 15 minutes

**Servings**: 4

## Ingredients:

- White vinegar, 1 tbsp.
- Salt
- Olive oil, 2 tbsps.
- Black pepper
- Lemon stevia, ¼ tsp.
- Juice from 2 limes
- Mashed avocados, 2
- Chopped onion, ¼ c.
- Chopped cilantro, ¼ c.
- For coleslaw mix
- Salt, 1 tsp.
- Small red cabbage, ¼
- Shredded carrot, ½
- Lemon juice, ¼ c.
- Small green cabbage, ½
- Olive oil, ¼ c.
- Stevia, 1 tbsp.
- Zest of ½ lemon

## Directions:

1. Set the mixing bowl in place to make the coleslaw salad
2. Add the mashed avocado and onions to coat well
3. Combine the seasonings, lime juice, vinegar, stevia, and oil in another bowl.
4. Add the mixture to the salad, mix to coat evenly
5. Enjoy

## Nutrition:

Calories: 481, Fat: 42, Fiber: 12, Carbs: 26, Protein: 6

## Sherry watercress broth

**Preparation Time**: 20 minutes

**Cooking Time:** 15 minutes

**Servings**: 4

## Ingredients:

- Sherry - ¼ cup
- Watercress- 6½ cups
- Chicken stock- 6 cups
- Coconut aminos- 2 tsp.
- Whisked egg whites of 3 eggs
- Shallots: chopped- 3
- Sesame seeds- 2 tsp.
- Salt and pepper

## Directions:

1. Pour the stock into the pot and add sherry, coconut amino, salt and pepper and mix. Boil on medium heat.
2. Mix in watercress, shallots, and whisked whites and let boil.
3. Serve sprinkled with sesame seeds.

## Nutrition:

Calories- 73, carbs- 7, protein- 9, fiber- 2, fats- 7

# Creamed cheddar Radishes

**Preparation Time**: 35 minutes

**Cooking Time:** 15 minutes

**Servings**: 1

**Ingredients:**

- Black pepper
- Halved radishes, 7 oz.
- Bacon slices, 2
- Chopped green onion, 1 tbsp.
- Sour cream, 2 tbsps.
- Cayenne pepper powder
- Salt
- Grated cheddar cheese, 1 tbsp.

**Directions:**

1. Set the radishes in a saucepan then add water.
2. Let it boil for 10 minutes over medium heat then drain the water
3. Set your pan over medium-high heat to cook the bacon to a crispy texture.
4. Drain the excess grease in a paper towel and reserve
5. Set the same pan again over medium heat then stir-fry the radishes for seven minutes
6. Stir in the seasonings, sour cream, and cayenne pepper powder for 7 minutes
7. Serve with crumbled bacon topped with cheddar cheese

**Nutrition:**

Calories: 319, Fat: 25, Fiber: 3, Carbs: 8, Protein: 11

# Mustard Egg and Avocado Salad

**Preparation Time**: 17 minutes

**Cooking Time:** 15 minutes

**Servings**: 4

**Ingredients:**

- Salt
- Mayonnaise, ¼ c.
- Medium eggs, 4
- Sliced avocado, 1
- Mustard, 2 tsps.
- Mixed lettuce leaves, 4 c.
- Chopped chives, 1 tbsp.
- Black pepper
- Minced garlic cloves, 2

**Directions:**

1. Set the cooking pan over medium-high heat.
2. Add water, eggs, and salt then allow to boil for about 7minutes.
3. Once boiled, drain the liquid, let cool then chop them.
4. Set a salad bowl in position to mix lettuce eggs and avocado
5. Toss with garlic, seasonings, and chives to coat
6. Combine the seasonings, mustard, and mayonnaise in another bowl
7. Add to the salad, toss and serve.

**Nutrition:**

Calories: 278, Fat: 16, Fiber: 7, Carbs: 13, Protein: 12

## Cucumber Avocado Salad mix

**Preparation Time**: 10 minutes

**Cooking Time:** 15 minutes

**Servings**: 4

**Ingredients:**

- Salt
- Sliced cucumber, 1
- Chopped avocados, 2
- Olive oil, 2 tbsps.
- Sliced onion, 1
- Chopped cilantro, ¼ c.
- Lemon juice, 2 tbsps.
- Black pepper
- Halved cherry tomatoes, 1 lb.

**Directions:**

1. Stir together cucumber, tomatoes, avocado, and onion in a salad bowl
2. Add the seasonings, lemon juice, and oil. Mix to coat well.
3. Serve cold topped with cilantro

**Nutrition:**

Calories: 310, Fat: 27, Fiber: 1, Carbs: 16, Protein: 8

**Fried Eggs with Kale and Bacon**

**Preparation Time** 5 minutes

**Cooking Time**: 15 minutes

**Servings**: 2

**Ingredients**

- 4 slices of turkey bacon, chopped
- 1 bunch of kale, chopped
- 3 oz. butter, unsalted
- 2 eggs
- 2 tbsp. chopped walnuts
- Seasoning:
- 1/3 tsp salt
- 1/3 tsp ground black pepper

**Directions:**

1. Take a frying pan, place it over medium heat, add two-third of the butter in it, and let it melt, then add kale, switch heat to medium-high level and cook for 4 to 5 minutes until edges have turned golden brown.
2. When done, transfer kale to a plate, set aside until required, add bacon into the pan and cook for 4 minutes until crispy.
3. Return kale into the pan, add nuts, stir until mixed and cook for 2 minutes until thoroughly warmed.
4. Transfer kale into the bowl, add remaining butter into the pan, crack eggs into the pan and fry them for 2 to 3 minutes until cooked to the desired level.
5. Distribute kale between two plates, add fried eggs on the side, sprinkle with salt and black pepper, and then serve.

**Nutrition**: 525 Calories; 50 g Fats; 14.4 g Protein; 1.1 g Net Carb; 2.8 g Fiber;

## Eggs with Greens

**Preparation Time**: 5 minutes

**Cooking Time**: 10 minutes;

**Servings**: 2

**Ingredients**

- 3 tbsp. chopped parsley
- 3 tbsp. chopped cilantro
- ¼ tsp cayenne pepper
- 2 eggs
- 1 tbsp. butter, unsalted
- Seasoning:
- ¼ tsp salt
- 1/8 tsp ground black pepper

**Directions:**

1. Take a medium skillet pan, place it over medium-low heat, add butter and wait until it melts.
2. Then add parsley and cilantro, season with salt and black pepper, stir until mixed and cook for 1 minute.
3. Make two space in the pan, crack an egg into each space, and then sprinkle with cayenne pepper, cover the pan with the lid and cook for 2 to 3 minutes until egg yolks have set.
4. Serve.

**Nutrition**: 135 Calories; 11.1 g Fats; 7.2 g Protein; 0.2 g Net Carb; 0.5 g Fiber;

## Spicy Chaffle with Jalapeno

**Preparation Time**: 5 minutes

**Cooking Time**: 10 minutes;

**Servings**: 2

**Ingredients**

- 2 tsp coconut flour
- ½ tbsp. chopped jalapeno pepper
- 2 tsp cream cheese
- 1 egg
- 2 oz. shredded mozzarella cheese
- Seasoning:
- ¼ tsp salt
- 1/8 tsp ground black pepper

## Directions:

1. Switch on a mini waffle maker and let it preheat for 5 minutes.
2. Meanwhile, take a medium bowl, place all the ingredients in it and then mix by using an immersion blender until smooth.
3. Ladle the batter evenly into the waffle maker, shut with lid, and let it cook for 3 to 4 minutes until firm and golden brown.
4. Serve.

**Nutrition**: 153 Calories; 10.7 g Fats; 11.1 g Protein; 1 g Net Carb; 1 g Fiber;

## Bulletproof Tea

**Preparation Time**: 5 minutes

**Cooking Time**: 0 minutes

**Servings**: 2

### Ingredients

- ¼ tsp cinnamon
- 2 cups strong tea
- 2 tbsp. coconut oil
- 2 tbsp. coconut milk

### Directions:

1. Distribute tea between two mugs, add remaining ingredients evenly and then stir until blended.
2. Serve.

**Nutrition**: 151 Calories; 17 g Fats; 0 g Protein; 1 g Net Carb; 0 g Fiber;

## Tea with Coconut

**Preparation Time**: 10 minutes

**Cooking Time**: 0 minutes;

**Servings** 2

**Ingredients**

- 2 tea bags, cinnamon-flavored
- 2 tbsp. MCT oil
- ¼ cup coconut milk, unsweetened
- 2 cups boiling water

### Directions:

1. Pour boiling water between two mugs, add a tea into each mug and let them steep for 5 minutes.
2. Meanwhile, take a small saucepan, place it over medium heat, pour in milk and heat for 3 minutes or more until hot.
3. After 5 minutes, remove tea bags from mugs, stir in milk, and MCT oil by using a milk frother until combined and then serve.

**Nutrition**: 191 Calories; 16 g Fats; 11 g Protein; 2 g Net Carb; 0 g Fiber;

# Cauliflower and Egg Plate

**Preparation Time**: 5 minutes

**Cooking Time**: 12 minutes;

**Servings**: 2

### Ingredients

- 4 oz. cauliflower florets, chopped
- 1 jalapeno pepper, sliced
- 2 eggs
- 1 ½ tbsp. avocado oil
- Seasoning:
- ¼ tsp salt
- 1/8 tsp ground black pepper

## Directions:

1. Take a skillet pan, place it over medium heat, add oil and when hot, add cauliflower florets and jalapeno and then cook for 5 to 7 minutes until tender.
2. Make two spaces in the pan, crack an egg in each space, and then cook for 3 to 4 minutes until eggs have cooked to the desired level.
3. When done, sprinkle salt and black pepper over eggs and then serve.

**Nutrition**: 191 Calories; 16 g Fats; 11 g Protein; 2 g Net Carb; 0 g Fiber

## Butternut Squash and Green Onions with Eggs

**Preparation Time**: 5 minutes

**Cooking Time**: 8 minutes;

**Servings**: 2

### Ingredients

- 4 oz. butternut squash pieces
- 1 green onion, sliced
- ½ tbsp. butter, unsalted
- 2 tsp grated parmesan cheese
- 2 eggs
- Seasoning:
- ¼ tsp salt
- ¼ tsp ground black pepper
- 1 tsp avocado oil

### Directions:

1. Take a skillet pan, place it over medium heat, add butter and oil and when hot, add butternut squash and green onion, season with 1/8 tsp of each salt and black pepper, stir until mixed and cook for 3 to 5 minutes until tender.
2. Make two space in the pan, crack an egg in each space, and sprinkle with cheese, season with remaining salt and black pepper, cover with the lid and cook for 2 to 3 minutes until the egg has cooked to the desired level.
3. Serve.

**Nutrition**: 191 Calories; 16 g Fats; 11 g Protein; 2 g Net Carb; 0 g Fiber

## Broccoli, Asparagus and Cheese Frittata

**Preparation Time**: 5 minutes

**Cooking Time**: 16 minutes;

**Servings**: 2

### Ingredients

- ¼ cup chopped broccoli florets
- 1-ounce asparagus spear cuts
- ½ tsp garlic powder
- 2 tbsp. whipping cream
- 2 eggs
- Seasoning:
- 2 tsp tbsp. avocado oil
- 1/8 tsp salt
- 1/8 tsp ground black pepper

### Directions:

1. Turn on the oven, then set it to 350 degrees F and let it preheat.
2. Take a medium bowl, crack eggs in it, add salt, black pepper and cream, whisk until combined and then stir in cheese, set aside until required.
3. Take a medium skillet pan, place it over medium heat, add oil and when hot, add broccoli florets and asparagus, sprinkle with garlic powder, stir until mixed and cook for 3 to 4 minutes until tender.
4. Spread the vegetables evenly in the pan, pour egg mixture over them and cook for 1 to 2 minutes until the mixture begins to firm.
5. Transfer the pan into the oven and then cook for 10 to 12 minutes until frittata has cooked and the top has turned golden brown.
6. When done, cut the frittata into slices and then serve.

**Nutrition**: 206 Calories; 17 g Fats; 10 g Protein; 2 g Net Carb; 1 g Fiber;

## Broccoli and Egg Plate

**Preparation Time**: 5 minutes

**Cooking Time**: 5 minutes;

**Servings**: 2

### Ingredients

- 3 oz. broccoli florets, chopped
- 2 eggs
- 1 tbsp. avocado oil
- ¼ tsp salt
- 1/8 tsp ground black pepper

**Directions:**

1. Take a heatproof bowl, place broccoli florets in it, cover with a plastic wrap, microwave for 2 minutes, and then drain well.
2. Take a medium skillet pan, place it over medium heat, add oil and when hot, add broccoli florets and cook for 2 minutes until golden brown.
3. Spread broccoli florets evenly in the pan crack eggs in the pan, sprinkle with salt and black pepper, cover with the lid and cook for 2 to 3 minutes until eggs have cooked to the desired level.
4. Serve.

**Nutrition**: 155 Calories; 12 g Fats; 8 g Protein; 1.6 g Net Carb; 1 g Fiber;

## Radish with Fried Eggs

**Preparation Time**: 5 minutes

**Cooking Time**: 10 minutes;

**Servings**: 2

### Ingredients

- ½ bunch of radish, diced
- ½ tsp garlic powder
- 1 tbsp. butter
- 1 tbsp. avocado oil
- 2 eggs
- Seasoning:
- 1/3 tsp salt
- ¼ tsp ground black pepper

**Directions:**

1. Take a medium skillet pan, place it over medium heat, add butter and when it melts, add radish, sprinkle with garlic powder and ¼ tsp salt and cook for 5 minutes until tender.
2. Distribute radish between two plates, then return pan over medium heat, add oil and when hot, crack eggs in it and fry for 2 to 3 minutes until cooked to desired level.
3. Add eggs to the radish and then serve.

**Nutrition**: 187 Calories; 17 g Fats; 7 g Protein; 0.4 g Net Carb; 0.5 g Fiber;

## Sunny Side Up Eggs on Creamed Spinach

**Preparation Time**: 5 minutes

**Cooking Time**: 10 minutes;

**Servings**: 2

### Ingredients

- 4 oz. of spinach leaves
- 1 tbsp. mustard paste
- 4 tbsp. whipping cream
- 2 eggs
- Seasoning:

- ¼ tsp salt
- ¼ tsp ground black pepper
- ½ tsp dried thyme
- 1 tbsp. avocado oil

### Directions:

1. Take a medium skillet pan, place it over high heat, pour in water to cover its bottom, then add spinach, toss until mixed and cook for 2 minutes until spinach wilts.
2. Then drain the spinach by passing it through a sieve placed on a bowl and set it aside.
3. Take a medium saucepan, place it over medium heat, add spinach, mustard, thyme, and cream, stir until mixed and cook for 2 minutes.
4. Then sprinkle black pepper over spinach, stir until mixed and remove the pan from heat.
5. Take a medium skillet pan, place it over medium-high heat, add oil and when hot, crack eggs in it and fry for 3 to 4 minutes until eggs have cooked to the desired level.
6. Divide spinach mixture evenly between two plates, top with a fried egg and then serve.

**Nutrition**: 280 Calories; 23.3 g Fats; 10.2 g Protein; 2.7 g Net Carb; 2.8 g Fiber;

## Creamy Kale Baked Eggs

**Preparation Time**: 10 minutes

**Cooking Time**: 20 minutes

**Servings**: 2

### Ingredients

- 1 bunch of kale, chopped
- 1-ounce grape tomatoes, halved
- 3 tbsp. whipping cream
- 2 tbsp. sour cream
- 2 eggs
- Seasoning:
- ½ tsp salt
- ½ tsp ground black pepper
- ½ tsp Italian seasoning
- 1 ½ tbsp. butter, unsalted

## Directions:

1. Turn on the oven, then set it to 400 degrees F and let it preheat.
2. Meanwhile, take a medium skillet pan, place butter in it, add butter and when it melts, add kale and cook for 2 minutes until wilted
3. Add Italian seasoning, 1/3 tsp each of salt and black pepper, cream and sour cream, then stir until mixed and cook for2 minutes until cheese has melted and the kale has thickened slightly.
4. Take two ramekins, divide creamed kale evenly between them, then top with cherry tomatoes and carefully crack an egg into each ramekin.
5. Sprinkle remaining salt and black pepper on eggs and then bake for 15 minutes until eggs have cooked completely.
6. Serve.

**Nutrition**: 301.5 Calories; 25.5 g Fats; 9.8 g Protein; 4.3 g Net Carb; 4 g Fiber;

## Butter Asparagus with Creamy Eggs

**Preparation Time**: 5 minutes

**Cooking Time**: 8 minutes;

**Servings**: 2

### Ingredients

- 4 oz. asparagus
- 2 eggs, blended
1. oz. grated parmesan cheese
- 1-ounce sour cream
- 2 tbsp. butter, unsalted
- Seasoning:
- 1/3 tsp salt
- 1/8 tsp ground black pepper
- ¼ tsp cayenne pepper
- ½ tbsp. avocado oil

**Directions:**

1. Take a medium skillet pan, place it over medium heat, add butter and when it melts, add blended eggs and then cook for 2 to 3 minutes until scrambled to the desired level; don't overcook.
2. Spoon the scrambled eggs into a food processor, add 1/8 tsp salt, cayenne pepper, sour cream and cheese and then pulse for 1 minute until smooth.
3. Return skillet pan over medium heat, add oil and when hot, add asparagus, season with black pepper and remaining salt, toss until mixed and cook for 3 minutes or more until roasted.
4. Distribute asparagus between two plates, add egg mixture, and then serve.

**Nutrition**: 338 Calories; 28.5 g Fats; 14.4 g Protein; 4.7 g Net Carb; 1.2 g Fiber;

## Spinach Egg Muffins

**Preparation Time**: 5 minutes

**Cooking Time**: 10 minutes;

**Servings**: 2

### Ingredients

- ½ cups chopped spinach
- 1/8 tsp dried basil
- 1/8 tsp garlic powder
- 2 large eggs
- 3 tbsp. grated Parmesan cheese
- Seasoning:
- ¼ tsp of sea salt
- 1/8 tsp ground black pepper

### Directions:

1. Turn on the oven, then set it to 400 degrees F, and let preheat.
2. Meanwhile, place eggs in a bowl, season with salt and black pepper and whisk until blended.
3. Add garlic and basil, whisk in mixed and then stir in spinach and cheese until combined.
4. Take two silicone muffin cups, grease them with reserved bacon greased, fill them evenly with prepared egg mixture and bake for 8 to 10 minutes until the top has nicely browned.
5. Serve.

**Nutrition**: 55 Calories; 3.5 g Fats; 4.5 g Protein; 0.4 g Net Carb; 0.2 g Fiber;

## Broccoli and Egg Muffin

**Preparation Time**: 10 minutes;

**Cooking Time**: 10 minutes

**Servings**: 2

**Ingredients**

- ¼ cup broccoli florets, steamed, chopped
- 2 tbsp. grated cheddar cheese
- 1/16 tsp dried thyme
- 1/16 tsp garlic powder
- 1 egg
- Seasoning:
- ¼ tsp salt
- 1/8 tsp ground black pepper

**Directions:**

1. Turn on the oven, then set it to 400 degrees F and let it preheat.
2. Meanwhile, take two silicone muffin cups, grease them with oil, and evenly fill them with broccoli and cheese.
3. Crack the egg in a bowl, add garlic powder, thyme, salt, and black pepper, whisk well, then evenly pour the mixture into muffin cups and bake for 8 to 10 minutes until done.
4. Serve.

**Nutrition**: 76 Calories; 5.1 g Fats; 5.7 g Protein; 1.2 g Net Carb; 0.7 g Fiber;

# Jalapeno and Cheese Egg Muffins

**Preparation Time**: 10 minutes

**Cooking Time**: 15 minutes

**Servings**: 2

## Ingredients

- 1 jalapeno pepper, diced
- 2 tbsp. sliced green onions
- 2 tbsp. grated parmesan cheese
- 1 tsp all-purpose seasoning
- 2 eggs
- Seasoning:
- 1/3 tsp salt
- ¼ tsp ground black pepper

## Directions:

1. Turn on the oven, then set it to 375 degrees F, and let it preheat.
2. Meanwhile, take two silicone muffin cups, grease with oil, and evenly fill them with cheese, jalapeno pepper, and green onion.
3. Crack eggs in a bowl, season with salt, black pepper, and all-purpose seasoning, whisk well, then evenly pour the mixture into muffin cups and bake for 15 to 20 minutes or until the top is slightly brown and muffins have puffed up.
4. Serve.

**Nutrition**: 108 Calories; 7.1 g Fats; 8.9 g Protein; 1.8 g Net Carb; 0.4 g Fiber;

# Cheesy Tomato and Olive Muffins

**Preparation Time**: 10 minutes

**Cooking Time**: 12 minutes;

**Servings**: 2

**Ingredients**

- 4 1/3 tbsp. almond flour
- ½ tbsp. coconut flour
- 1/3 tbsp. chopped tomato
- 1/3 tbsp. sliced green olives
- 2 tbsp. sour cream
- Seasoning:
- 1/8 tsp baking powder
- 2/3 tbsp. avocado oil
- 3 tbsp. grated parmesan cheese
- ½ of egg

**Directions:**

1. Turn on the oven, then set it to 320 degrees F and let it preheat.
2. Meanwhile, take a medium bowl, place flours in it, and stir in the baking powder until mixed.
3. Add eggs along with sour cream and oil, whisk until blended and then fold in cheese, tomato, and olives until just mixed.
4. Take two silicone muffin cups, add the prepared batter in it evenly and then bake for 10 to 12 minutes until cooked but slightly moist in the middle.
5. When done, let muffin cools for 5 minutes, then take them out and serve.

**Nutrition**: 256 Calories; 23.5 g Fats; 8.7 g Protein; 1 g Net Carb; 1.8 g Fiber;

## Buttery Broccoli and Bacon

**Preparation Time**: 5 minutes;

**Cooking Time**: 12 minutes;

**Servings**: 2

### Ingredients

1 slice of turkey bacon

1 cup chopped broccoli florets

1/8 tsp garlic powder

¼ tsp Italian seasoning

¼ tbsp. unsalted butter

Seasoning:

1/8 tsp salt

1/8 tsp ground black pepper

### Directions:

1. Take a medium skillet pan, place it over high heat, add bacon slice and cook for 3 to 5 minutes until crispy.
2. Transfer bacon to a cutting board and then chop it into small pieces.
3. Reduce the heat to medium-low level, add broccoli florets into the pan, stir well into the bacon grease, add butter, then toss until mixed and cook for 5 minutes until tender.
4. Season the broccoli florets with salt, black pepper, and Italian seasoning, add chopped bacon, stir well and cook for 2 minutes until thoroughly heated.
5. Serve.

**Nutrition**: 77 Calories; 5 g Fats; 5 g Protein; 1 g Net Carb; 2 g Fiber;

**Broccoli Salad with Bacon**

**Preparation Time**: 5 minutes;

**Cooking Time**: 0 minutes;

**Servings**: 2

**Ingredients**

- 1 cup broccoli florets, chopped
- 4 tbsp. whipped topping
- 2 tbsp. shredded cheddar cheese
- 3 slices of turkey bacon, cooked, chopped
- 1/3 tsp garlic powder
- Seasoning:
- 1/8 tsp salt
- 1/8 tsp dried parsley

**Directions:**

1. Take a medium bowl, place whipped topping in it, whisk in garlic powder and parsley, and then fold in broccoli florets.
2. Top with bacon and cheddar cheese and serve.

**Nutrition**: 119 Calories; 10 g Fats; 3.5 g Protein; 2 g Net Carb; 0.5 g Fiber;

## Roasted Green Beans

**Preparation Time**: 5 minutes

**Cooking Time**: 25 minutes;

**Servings**: 2

**Ingredients**

- ½ pound green beans
- ½ cup grated parmesan cheese
- 3 tbsp. coconut oil
- ½ tsp garlic powder
- Seasoning:
- 1/3 tsp salt
- 1/8 tsp ground black pepper

## Directions:

1. Turn on the oven, then set it to 425 degrees F, and let preheat.
2. Take a baking sheet, line green beans on it, and set aside until required.
3. Prepare the dressing, and for this, place remaining ingredients in a bowl, except for cheese and whisk until combined.
4. Drizzle the dressing over green beans, toss until well coated, and then bake for 20 minutes until green beans are tender-crisp.
5. Then sprinkle cheese on top of beans and continue roasting for 3 to 5 minutes or until cheese melts and nicely golden brown.
6. Serve.

**Nutrition**: 119 Calories; 9 g Fats; 5 g Protein; 4.5 g Net Carb; 3 g Fiber;

## Fried Cauliflower and Egg Rice

**Preparation Time**: 5 minutes;

**Cooking Time**: 12 minutes

**Servings**: 2

**Ingredients**

- 8-ounce cauliflower florets, riced
- 2 green onion, sliced
- 1 large egg, beaten
- 1 tbsp. soy sauce
- ½ tsp toasted sesame oil
- Seasoning:
- 1 tbsp. coconut oil
- ½ tsp garlic powder

**Directions:**

1. Take a large skillet pan, place it over medium-high heat, add coconut oil and riced cauliflower, and cook for 5 minutes until softened.
2. Then add green onions, stir well and cook for 3 minutes until onions are tender.
3. Season with salt, sprinkle garlic over cauliflower, cook for 1 minute until fragrant, then pour in the egg, stir well and cook for 2 minutes until the egg has scrambled to desire level, stirring continuously.
4. Drizzle with soy sauce and sesame oil and Serve.

**Nutrition**: 57 Calories; 4 g Fats; 3 g Protein; 1.7 g Net Carb; 0.5 g Fiber

## Spinach Zucchini Boats

**Preparation Time**: 5 minutes

**Cooking Time**: 10 minutes;

**Servings**: 2

### Ingredients

- 1 large zucchini
- ¾ cup spinach
- 1 ½ tbsp. whipped topping
- 3 tbsp. grated parmesan cheese
- ½ tsp garlic powder
- Seasoning:
- ½ tsp salt
- ½ tsp ground black pepper

### Directions:

1. Turn on the oven, then set it to 350 degrees F, and let preheat.
2. Take a skillet pan, place it over medium heat, add spinach and cook for 5 to 7 minutes or until spinach leaves have wilted and their moisture has evaporated completely.
3. Sprinkle garlic powder, ¼ tsp each of salt and black pepper over spinach, add whipped topping and 2 tbsp. cheese and stir well until the cheese has melted, remove the pan from heat.
4. Cut off the top and bottom of zucchini, then cut it in half lengthwise and make a well by scooping out pulp along the center, leaving ½-inch shell.
5. Season zucchini with remaining salt and black pepper, place them on a baking sheet and roast for 5 minutes.
6. Then fill zucchini evenly with spinach mixture, top with remaining cheese and broil for 3 minutes until cheese has melted.
7. Serve.

**Nutrition**: 86.5 Calories; 6 g Fats; 4 g Protein; 3.5 g Net Carb; 0.5 g Fiber;

# Green Beans with Herbs

**Preparation Time**: 5 minutes

**Cooking Time**: 7 minutes;

**Servings**: 2

## Ingredients

- 3 oz. green beans
- 2 slices of bacon, diced
- 3 tbsp. chopped parsley
- 3 tbsp. chopped cilantro
- 1 tbsp. avocado oil
- Seasoning:
- ½ tsp garlic powder
- ¼ tsp salt

## Directions:

1. Place green beans in a medium heatproof bowl, cover with a plastic wrap, and then microwave for 3 to 4 minutes at high heat setting until tender.
2. Meanwhile, take a medium skillet pan, place it over medium heat and when hot, add bacon and cook for 3 to 4 minutes until crisp.
3. Season bacon with salt, sprinkle with garlic powder and cook for 30 seconds until fragrant, remove the pan from heat.
4. When green beans have steamed, drain them well, rinse under cold water, and then transfer to a bowl.
5. Add bacon and remaining ingredients and toss until well mixed.
6. Serve.

**Nutrition**: 380 Calories; 33.7 g Fats; 15.2 g Protein; 2.4 g Net Carb; 1.4 g Fiber;

## Salad Sandwiches

**Preparation Time**: 5 minutes;

**Cooking Time**: 0 minutes;

**Servings**: 2

### Ingredients

- 1 medium avocado, peeled, pitted, diced
- 2 leaves of iceberg lettuce
- 1-ounce unsalted butter
- 2-ounce cheddar cheese, sliced

### Directions:

1. Rinse the lettuce leaves, pat dry with a paper towel, and then smear each leaf with butter.
2. Top lettuce with cheese and avocado and serve.

**Nutrition:** 187 Calories; 17 g Fats; 5 g Protein; 4 g Net Carb; 1.5 g Fiber;

## Celeriac Stuffed Avocado

**Preparation Time**: 10 minutes;

**Cooking Time**: 0 minutes

**Servings**: 2

**Ingredients**

- 1 avocado
- 1 celery root, finely chopped
- 2 tbsp. mayonnaise
- ½ of a lemon, juiced, zested
- 2 tbsp. mayonnaise
- Seasoning:
- ¼ tsp salt

**Directions:**

1. Prepare avocado and for this, cut avocado in half and then remove its pit.
2. Place remaining ingredients in a bowl, stir well until combined and evenly stuff this mixture into avocado halves.
3. Serve.

**Nutrition**: 285 Calories; 27 g Fats; 2.8 g Protein; 4.4 g Net Carb; 2.6 g Fiber;

## Cobb salad

**Preparation Time**: 5 minutes

**Cooking Time**: 10 minutes;

**Servings**: 1

### Ingredients

- 1 large egg, hard-boiled, peeled, diced
- 2 oz. chicken thigh
- 2 1/2 slices bacon, cooked, crumbled
- ½ of a medium avocado, diced
- ½ cup chopped lettuce

- Seasoning:
- 1 cup of water
- 3 tbsp. apple cider vinegar
- 1 ½ tbsp. coconut oil
- ¼ tsp salt
- 1/8 tsp ground black pepper

**Directions:**

1. Cook chicken thigh and for this, place chicken thighs in an instant pot, pour in 1 cup water, and shut the pot with a lid.
2. Cook the chicken for 5 minutes at high pressure, and when done, let the pressure release naturally.
3. Meanwhile, cook the bacon and for this, take a skillet pan, place it over medium heat and when hot, add bacon slices.
4. Cook the bacon for 3 to 5 minutes until golden brown, then transfer them to a cutting board and chop the bacon, reserve the bacon grease in the pan for the next meal.
5. When chicken thigh has cooked, transfer it to a bowl and shred the chicken with two forks, reserving the chicken broth for later use.

6. Assemble the salad and for this, place lettuce in a salad plate, top with chicken, bacon, diced eggs, avocado, and chicken in horizontal rows.
7. Prepare the dressing and for this, whisk together salt, black pepper, vinegar, and oil until incorporated and then drizzle the dressing generously over the salad.
8. Serve.

**Nutrition**: 206 Calories; 11.8 g Fats; 19.2 g Protein; 6 g Net Carb; 3 g Fiber;

# Poultry

## Pancakes

**Preparation Time**: 5 minutes

**Cooking Time**: 6 minutes

**Servings**: 2

**Ingredients**

- ¼ cup almond flour
- 1 ½ tbsp. unsalted butter
- 2 oz. cream cheese, softened
- 2 eggs

### Directions:

1. Take a bowl, crack eggs in it, whisk well until fluffy, and then whisk in flour and cream cheese until well combined.
2. Take a skillet pan, place it over medium heat, add butter and when it melts, drop pancake batter in four sections, spread it evenly, and cook for 2 minutes per side until brown.
3. Serve.

**Nutrition**: 166.8 Calories; 15 g Fats; 5.8 g Protein; 1.8 g Net Carb; 0.8 g Fiber;

## Cheese Roll-Ups

**Preparation Time**: 5 minutes

**Cooking Time**: 0 minutes;

**Servings**: 2

### Ingredients

- 2 oz. mozzarella cheese, sliced, full-fat
- 1-ounce butter, unsalted

### Directions:

1. Cut cheese into slices and then cut butter into thin slices.
2. Top each cheese slice with a slice of butter, roll it and then serve.

**Nutrition**: 166 Calories; 15 g Fats; 6.5 g Protein; 2 g Net Carb; 0 g Fiber;

## Scrambled Eggs with Spinach and Cheese

**Preparation Time**: 5 minutes

**Cooking Time**: 5 minutes;

**Servings**: 2

### Ingredients

- 2 oz. spinach
- 2 eggs
- 1 tbsp. coconut oil
- 2 tbsp. grated mozzarella cheese, full-fat
- Seasoning:
- ¼ tsp salt
- 1/8 tsp ground black pepper
- 1/8 tsp red pepper flakes

### Directions:

1. Take a medium bowl, crack eggs in it, add salt and black pepper and whisk until combined.
2. Take a medium skillet pan, place it over medium heat, add oil, add spinach and cook for 1 minute until leaves wilt.
3. Pour eggs over spinach, stir and cook for 1 minute until just set.
4. Stir in cheese, then remove the pan from heat and sprinkle red pepper flakes on top.
5. Serve.

**Nutrition**: 171 Calories; 14 g Fats; 9.2 g Protein; 1.1 g Net Carb; 1.7 g Fiber;

**Egg Wraps**

**Preparation Time**: 5 minutes

**Cooking Time**: 5 minutes;

**Servings**: 2

**Ingredients**

- 2 eggs
- 1 tbsp. coconut oil
- Seasoning:
- ¼ tsp salt
- 1/8 tsp ground black pepper

**Directions:**

Take a medium bowl, crack eggs in it, add salt and black pepper, and then whisk until blended.

Take a frying pan, place it over medium-low heat, add coconut oil and when it melts, pour in half of the egg, spread it evenly into a thin layer by rotating the pan and cook for 2 minutes.

Then flip the pan, cook for 1 minute, and transfer to a plate.

Repeat with the remaining egg to make another wrap, then roll each egg wrap and serve.

**Nutrition**: 68 Calories; 4.7 g Fats; 5.5 g Protein; 0.5 g Net Carb; 0 g Fiber;

## Chaffles with Poached Eggs

**Preparation Time**: 5 minutes

**Cooking Time**: 10 minutes;

**Servings**: 2

### Ingredients

- 2 tsp coconut flour
- ½ cup shredded cheddar cheese, full-fat
- 3 eggs
- Seasoning:
- ¼ tsp salt
- 1/8 tsp ground black pepper

**Directions:**

1. Switch on a mini waffle maker and let it preheat for 5 minutes.
2. Meanwhile, take a medium bowl, place all the ingredients in it, reserving 2 eggs and then mix by using an immersion blender until smooth.
3. Spoon the batter evenly into the waffle maker, shut with lid, and let it cook for 3 to 4 minutes until firm and golden brown.
4. Meanwhile, prepare poached eggs, and for this, take a medium bowl half full with water, place it over medium heat and bring it to a boil.
5. Then crack an egg in a ramekin, carefully pour it into the boiling water and cook for 3 minutes.
6. Transfer egg to a plate lined with paper towels using a slotted spoon and repeat with the other egg.
7. Top chaffles with poached eggs, season with salt and black pepper, and then serve.

**Nutrition**: 265 Calories; 18.5 g Fats; 17.6 g Protein; 3.4 g Net Carb; 6 g Fiber;

## Chaffle with Scrambled Eggs

**Preparation Time**: 5 minutes

**Cooking Time**: 10 minutes;

**Servings: 2**

**Ingredients**

- 2 tsp coconut flour
- ½ cup shredded cheddar cheese, full-fat
- 3 eggs
- 1-ounce butter, unsalted
- Seasoning:
- ¼ tsp salt
- 1/8 tsp ground black pepper
- 1/8 tsp dried oregano

**Directions:**

1. Switch on a mini waffle maker and let it preheat for 5 minutes.
2. Meanwhile, take a medium bowl, place all the ingredients in it, reserving 2 eggs and then mix by using an immersion blender until smooth.
3. Spoon the batter evenly into the waffle maker, shut with lid, and let it cook for 3 to 4 minutes until firm and golden brown.
4. Meanwhile, prepare scrambled eggs and for this, take a medium bowl, crack the eggs in it and whisk them with a fork until frothy, and then season with salt and black pepper.
5. Take a medium skillet pan, place it over medium heat, add butter and when it melts, pour in eggs and cook for 2 minutes until creamy, stirring continuously.
6. Top chaffles with scrambled eggs, sprinkle with oregano, and then serve.

**Nutrition**: 265 Calories; 18.5 g Fats; 17.6 g Protein; 3.4 g Net Carb; 6 g Fiber;

## Sheet Pan Eggs with Mushrooms and Spinach

**Preparation Time**: 5 minutes

**Cooking Time**: 12 minutes;

**Servings**: 2

### Ingredients

- 2 eggs
- 1 tsp chopped jalapeno pepper
- 1 tbsp. chopped mushrooms
- 1 tbsp. chopped spinach
- 1 tbsp. chopped chard
- Seasoning:
- 1/3 tsp salt
- 1/4 tsp ground black pepper

### Directions:

1. Turn on the oven, then set it to 350 degrees F and let it preheat.
2. Take a medium bowl, crack eggs in it, add salt and black pepper, then add all the vegetables and stir until combined.
3. Take a medium sheet ball or rimmed baking sheet, grease it with oil, pour prepared egg batter on it, and then bake for 10 to 12 minutes until done.
4. Cut egg into two squares and then serve.

**Nutrition**: 165 Calories; 10.7 g Fats; 14 g Protein; 1.5 g Net Carb; 0.5 g Fiber;

## No Bread Breakfast Sandwich

**Preparation Time**: 10 minutes

**Cooking Time**: 15 minutes;

**Servings**: 2

### Ingredients

- 2 slices of ham
- 4 eggs
- 1 tsp tabasco sauce
- 3 tbsp. butter, unsalted
- 2 tsp grated mozzarella cheese
- Seasoning:
- ¼ tsp salt
- 1/8 tsp ground black pepper

### Directions:

1. Take a frying pan, place it over medium heat, add butter and when it melt, crack an egg in it and fry for 2 to 3 minutes until cooked to desired level.
2. Transfer fried egg to a plate, fry remaining eggs in the same manner and when done, season eggs with salt and black pepper.
3. Prepare the sandwich and for this, use a fried egg as a base for sandwich, then top with a ham slice, sprinkle with a tsp of ham and cover with another fried egg.
4. Place egg into the pan, return it over low heat and let it cook until cheese melts.
5. Prepare another sandwich in the same manner and then serve.

**Nutrition**: 180 Calories; 15 g Fats; 10 g Protein; 1 g Net Carb; 0 g Fiber;

## Scrambled Eggs with Basil and Butter

**Preparation Time**: 5 minutes

**Cooking Time**: 5 minutes;

**Servings**: 2

### Ingredients

- 1 tbsp. chopped basil leaves
- 2 tbsp. butter, unsalted
- 2 tbsp. grated cheddar cheese
- 2 eggs
- 2 tbsp. whipping cream
- Seasoning:
- 1/8 tsp salt
- 1/8 tsp ground black pepper

### Directions:

1. Take a medium bowl, crack eggs in it, add salt, black pepper, cheese and cream and whisk until combined.
2. Take a medium pan, place it over low heat, add butter and when it melts, pour in the egg mixture and cook for 2 to 3 minutes until eggs have scrambled to the desired level.
3. When done, distribute scrambled eggs between two plates, top with basil leaves and then serve.

**Nutrition**: 320 Calories; 29 g Fats; 13 g Protein; 1.5 g Net Carb; 0 g Fiber;

**Bacon, and Eggs**

**Preparation Time**: 5 minutes

**Cooking Time**: 10 minutes;

**Servings**: 2

**Ingredients**

- 2 eggs
- 4 slices of turkey bacon
- ¼ tsp salt
- ¼ tsp ground black pepper

**Directions:**

1. Take a skillet pan, place it over medium heat, add bacon slices, and cook for 5 minutes until crispy.
2. Transfer bacon slices to a plate and set aside until required, reserving the fat in the pan.
3. Cook the egg in the pan one at a time, and for this, crack an egg in the pan and cook for 2 to 3 minutes or more until the egg has cooked to desire level.
4. Transfer egg to a plate and cook the other egg in the same manner.
5. Season eggs with salt and black pepper and then serve with cooked bacon.

**Nutrition**: 136 Calories; 11 g Fats; 7.5 g Protein; 1 g Net Carb; 0 g Fiber

## Boiled Eggs

**Preparation Time**: 5 minutes

**Cooking Time**: 10 minutes;

**Servings**: 2

### Ingredients

- 2 eggs
- ½ of a medium avocado
- Seasoning:
- ¼ tsp salt
- ¼ tsp ground black pepper

### Directions:

1. Place a medium pot over medium heat, fill it half full with water and bring it to boil.
2. Then carefully place the eggs in the boiling water and boil the eggs for 5 minutes until soft-boiled, 8 minutes for medium-boiled, and 10 minutes for hard-boiled.
3. When eggs have boiled, transfer them to a bowl containing chilled water and let them rest for 5 minutes.
4. Then crack the eggs with a spoon and peel them.
5. Cut each egg into slices, season with salt and black pepper, and serve with diced avocado.

**Nutrition**: 112 Calories; 9.5 g Fats; 5.5 g Protein; 1 g Net Carb; 0 g Fiber;

# Beef

**Beef and Broccoli**

**Preparation Time**: 5 minutes

**Cooking Time**: 10 minutes;

**Servings**: 2

**Ingredients**

- 6 slices of beef roast, cut into strips
- 1 scallion, chopped
- 3 oz. broccoli florets, chopped
- 1 tbsp. avocado oil
- 1 tbsp. butter, unsalted
- Seasoning:
- ¼ tsp salt
- 1/8 tsp ground black pepper
- 1 ½ tbsp. soy sauce
- 3 tbsp. chicken broth

**Directions:**

1. Take a medium skillet pan, place it over medium heat, add oil and when hot, add beef strips and cook for 2 minutes until hot.
2. Transfer beef to a plate, add scallion to the pan, then add butter and cook for 3 minutes until tender.
3. Add remaining ingredients, stir until mixed, switch heat to the low level and simmer for 3 to 4 minutes until broccoli is tender.
4. Return beef to the pan, stir until well combined and cook for 1 minute.
5. Serve.

**Nutrition**: 245 Calories; 15.7 g Fats; 21.6 g Protein; 1.7 g Net Carb; 1.3 g Fiber;

# Beef with Cabbage Noodles

**Preparation Time**: 5 minutes

**Cooking Time**: 18 minutes

**Servings**: 2

## Ingredients

- 4 oz. ground beef
- 1 cup chopped cabbage
- 4 oz. tomato sauce
- ½ tsp minced garlic
- ½ cup of water
- Seasoning:
- ½ tbsp. coconut oil
- ½ tsp salt
- ¼ tsp Italian seasoning
- 1/8 tsp dried basil

## Directions:

1. Take a skillet pan, place it over medium heat, add oil and when hot, add beef and cook for 5 minutes until nicely browned.
2. Meanwhile, prepare the cabbage and for it, slice the cabbage into thin shred.
3. When the beef has cooked, add garlic, season with salt, basil, and Italian seasoning, stir well and continue cooking for 3 minutes until beef has thoroughly cooked.
4. Pour in tomato sauce and water, stir well and bring the mixture to boil.
5. Then reduce heat to medium-low level, add cabbage, stir well until well mixed and simmer for 3 to 5 minutes until cabbage is softened, covering the pan.
6. Uncover the pan and continue simmering the beef until most of the cooking liquid has evaporated.
7. Serve.

**Nutrition**: 188.5 Calories; 12.5 g Fats; 15.5 g Protein; 2.5 g Net Carb; 1 g Fiber;

## Garlic Herb Beef Roast

**Preparation Time**: 5 minutes

**Cooking Time**: 10 minutes;

**Servings**: 2

### Ingredients

- 6 slices of beef roast
- ½ tsp garlic powder
- 1/3 tsp dried thyme
- ¼ tsp dried rosemary
- 2 tbsp. butter, unsalted
- Seasoning:
- 1/3 tsp salt
- 1/4 tsp ground black pepper

### Directions:

1. Prepare the spice mix and for this, take a small bowl, place garlic powder, thyme, rosemary, salt, and black pepper and then stir until mixed.
2. Sprinkle spice mix on the beef roast.
3. Take a medium skillet pan, place it over medium heat, add butter and when it melts, add beef roast and then cook for 5 to 8 minutes until golden brown and cooked.
4. Serve.

**Nutrition**: 140 Calories; 12.7 g Fats; 5.5 g Protein; 0.1 g Net Carb; 0.2 g Fiber;

## Garlicky Steaks with Rosemary

**Preparation Time**: 25 minutes

**Cooking Time**: 12 minutes;

**Servings**: 2

### Ingredients

- 2 beef steaks
- 1/4 of a lime, juiced
- 1 ½ tsp garlic powder
- ¾ tsp dried rosemary
- 2 ½ tbsp. avocado oil
- Seasoning:
- ½ tsp salt
- ¼ tsp ground black pepper

### Directions:

1. Prepare steaks, and for this, sprinkle garlic powder on all sides of steak.
2. Take a shallow dish, place 1 ½ tbsp. In it, oil and lime juice whisk until combined, add steaks, turn to coat, and let it marinate for 20 minutes at room temperature.
3. Then take a griddle pan, place it over medium-high heat and grease it with remaining oil.
4. Season marinated steaks with salt and black pepper, add to the griddle and cook for 7 to 12 minutes until cooked to the desired level.
5. When done, wrap steaks in foil for 5 minutes, then cut into slices across the grain.
6. Sprinkle rosemary over steaks slices and then serve.

**Nutrition**: 213 Calories; 13 g Fats; 22 g Protein; 1 g Net Carb; 0 g Fiber;

## Roast Beef and Mozzarella Plate

**Preparation Time**: 5 minutes

**Cooking Time**: 0 minutes;

**Servings**: 2

### Ingredients

- 4 slices of roast beef
- ½ ounce chopped lettuce
- 1 avocado, pitted
- 2 oz. mozzarella cheese, cubed
- ½ cup mayonnaise
- Seasoning:
- ¼ tsp salt
- 1/8 tsp ground black pepper
- 2 tbsp. avocado oil

### Directions:

1. Scoop out flesh from avocado and divide it evenly between two plates.
2. Add slices of roast beef, lettuce, and cheese and then sprinkle with salt and black pepper.
3. Serve with avocado oil and mayonnaise.

**Nutrition**: 267.7 Calories; 24.5 g Fats; 9.5 g Protein; 1.5 g Net Carb; 2 g Fiber;

## Sprouts Stir-fry with Kale, Broccoli, and Beef

**Preparation Time**: 5 minutes

**Cooking Time**: 8 minutes;

**Servings**: 2

**Ingredients**

- 3 slices of beef roast, chopped
- 2 oz. Brussels sprouts, halved
- 4 oz. broccoli florets
- 3 oz. kale
- 1 ½ tbsp. butter, unsalted
- 1/8 tsp red pepper flakes
- Seasoning:
- ¼ tsp garlic powder
- ¼ tsp salt
- 1/8 tsp ground black pepper

**Directions:**

1. Take a medium skillet pan, place it over medium heat, add ¾ tbsp. When it melts, add broccoli florets and sprouts, sprinkle with garlic powder, and cook for 2 minutes.
2. Season vegetables with salt and red pepper flakes, add chopped beef, stir until mixed and continue cooking for 3 minutes until browned on one side.
3. Then add kale and remaining butter, flip the vegetables and cook for 2 minutes until kale leaves wilts.
4. Serve.

**Nutrition**: 125 Calories; 9.4 g Fats; 4.8 g Protein; 1.7 g Net Carb; 2.6 g Fiber;

**Beef and Vegetable Skillet**

**Preparation Time**: 5 minutes

**Cooking Time**: 15 minutes

**Servings**: 2

**Ingredients**

- 3 oz. spinach, chopped
- ½ pound ground beef
- 2 slices of bacon, diced
- 2 oz. chopped asparagus
- Seasoning:
- 3 tbsp. coconut oil
- 2 tsp dried thyme
- 2/3 tsp salt
- ½ tsp ground black pepper

**Directions:**

1. Take a skillet pan, place it over medium heat, add oil and when hot, add beef and bacon and cook for 5 to 7 minutes until slightly browned.
2. Then add asparagus and spinach, sprinkle with thyme, stir well and cook for 7 to 10 minutes until thoroughly cooked.
3. Season skillet with salt and black pepper and serve.

**Nutrition**: 332.5 Calories; 26 g Fats; 23.5 g Protein; 1.5 g Net Carb; 1 g Fiber;

## Beef, Pepper and Green Beans Stir-fry

**Preparation Time**: 5 minutes;

**Cooking Time**: 18 minutes

**Servings**: 2

**Ingredients**

- 6 oz. ground beef
- 2 oz. chopped green bell pepper
- 4 oz. green beans
- 3 tbsp. grated cheddar cheese
- Seasoning:
- ½ tsp salt
- ¼ tsp ground black pepper
- ¼ tsp paprika

**Directions:**

1. Take a skillet pan, place it over medium heat, add ground beef and cook for 4 minutes until slightly browned.
2. Then add bell pepper and green beans, season with salt, paprika, and black pepper, stir well and continue cooking for 7 to 10 minutes until beef and vegetables have cooked through.
3. Sprinkle cheddar cheese on top, then transfer pan under the broiler and cook for 2 minutes until cheese has melted and the top is golden brown.
4. Serve.

**Nutrition**: 282.5 Calories; 17.6 g Fats; 26.1 g Protein; 2.9 g Net Carb; 2.1 g Fiber;

## Roast Beef and Vegetable Plate

**Preparation Time**: 10 minutes

**Cooking Time**: 10 minutes;

**Servings**: 2

### Ingredients

- 2 scallions, chopped in large pieces
- 1 ½ tbsp. coconut oil
- 4 thin slices of roast beef
- 4 oz. cauliflower and broccoli mix
- 1 tbsp. butter, unsalted
- Seasoning:
- 1/2 tsp salt
- 1/3 tsp ground black pepper
- 1 tsp dried parsley

## Directions:

1. Turn on the oven, then set it to 400 degrees F, and let it preheat.
2. Take a baking sheet, grease it with oil, place slices of roast beef on one side, and top with butter.
3. Take a separate bowl, add cauliflower and broccoli mix, add scallions, drizzle with oil, season with remaining salt and black pepper, toss until coated and then spread vegetables on the empty side the baking sheet.
4. Bake for 5 to 7 minutes until beef is nicely browned and vegetables are tender-crisp, tossing halfway.
5. Distribute beef and vegetables between two plates and then serve.

**Nutrition**: 313 Calories; 26 g Fats; 15.6 g Protein; 2.8 g Net Carb; 1.9 g Fiber;

## Cheesy Meatloaf

**Preparation Time**: 5 minutes

**Cooking Time**: 4 minutes

**Servings**: 2

### Ingredients

- 4 oz. ground turkey
- 1 egg
- 1 tbsp. grated mozzarella cheese
- ¼ tsp Italian seasoning
- ½ tbsp. soy sauce
- Seasoning:
- ¼ tsp salt
- 1/8 tsp ground black pepper

**Directions:**

1. Take a bowl, place all the ingredients in it, and stir until mixed.
2. Take a heatproof mug, spoon in prepared mixture and microwave for 3 minutes at high heat setting until cooked.
3. When done, let meatloaf rest in the mug for 1 minute, then take it out, cut it into two slices and serve.

**Nutrition**: 196.5 Calories; 13.5 g Fats; 18.7 g Protein; 18.7 g Net Carb; 0 g Fiber;

## Steak and Cheese Plate

**Preparation Time**: 5 minutes;

**Cooking Time**: 10 minutes;

**Servings**: 2

**Ingredients**

- 1 green onion, chopped
- 2 oz. chopped lettuce
- 2 beef steaks
- 2 oz. of cheddar cheese, sliced
- ½ cup mayonnaise
- Seasoning:
- ¼ tsp salt
- 1/8 tsp ground black pepper
- 3 tbsp. avocado oil

**Directions:**

1. Prepare the steak, and for this, season it with salt and black pepper.
2. Take a medium skillet pan, place it over medium heat, add oil and when hot, add seasoned steaks, and cook for 7 to 10 minutes until cooked to the desired level.
3. When done, distribute steaks between two plates, add scallion, lettuce, and cheese slices.
4. Drizzle with remaining oil and then serve with mayonnaise.

**Nutrition**: 714 Calories; 65.3 g Fats; 25.3 g Protein; 4 g Net Carb; 5.3 g Fiber;

# Beef Clod Vindaloo

**Preparation Time:** 15 minutes

**Cooking Time:** 15 minutes

**Servings:** 2

**Ingredients:**

- ½ Serrano pepper, chopped
- ¼ teaspoon cumin seeds
- ¼ teaspoon minced ginger
- ¼ teaspoon cayenne pepper
- ¼ teaspoon salt
- ¼ teaspoon ground paprika
- 1 cup water
- 9 ounces (255 g) beef clod, chopped

**Directions:**

1. Put Serrano pepper, cumin seeds, minced ginger, cayenne pepper, salt, ground paprika, and water in a food processor. Blend the mixture until smooth.
2. Transfer the mixture in a bowl and add the chopped beef clod. Toss to coat well.
3. Transfer the beef clod and the mixture in the Instant Pot and close the lid.
4. Select Manual mode and set cooking time for 15 minutes on High Pressure.
5. When timer beeps, use a natural pressure release for 10 minutes, then release any remaining pressure. Open the lid.
6. Serve immediately.

**Nutrition:**

Calories: 376

Fiber: 0.3g

Fat: 27.4g

Protein: 29.9g

Carbs: 0.7g

Net carbs: 0.4g

# Beef Masala Curry

**Preparation Time:** 10 minutes

**Cooking Time:** 20 minutes

**Servings:** 4

**Ingredients:**

- 2 tomatoes, quartered
- 1 small onion, quartered
- 4 garlic cloves, chopped
- ½ cup fresh cilantro leaves
- 1 teaspoon garam masala
- ½ teaspoon ground coriander
- 1 teaspoon ground cumin
- ½ teaspoon cayenne
- 1 teaspoon salt
- 1 pound (454 g) beef chuck roast, cut into 1-inch cubes

**Directions:**

1. In a blender, combine the tomatoes, onion, garlic, and cilantro.
2. Process until the vegetables are puréed. Add the garam masala, coriander, cumin, cayenne, and salt. Process for several more seconds.
3. To the Instant Pot, add the beef and pour the vegetable purée on top.
4. Lock the lid. Select Manual mode and set cooking time for 20 minutes on High Pressure.
5. When timer beeps, let the pressure release naturally for 10 minutes, then release any remaining pressure. Unlock the lid.
6. Stir and serve immediately.

**Nutrition:**

Calories: 309

Fat: 21.0g

Protein: 24.0g

Carbs: 6.0g

Net carbs: 4.0g

Fiber: 2.0g

# Beef Ribs with Radishes

**Preparation Time:** 20 minutes

**Cooking Time:** 56 minutes

**Servings:** 4

**Ingredients:**

- ¼ teaspoon ground coriander
- ¼ teaspoon ground cumin
- 1 teaspoon kosher salt, plus more to taste
- ½ teaspoon smoked paprika
- Pinch of ground allspice (optional)
- 4 (8-ounce / 227-g) bone-in beef short ribs
- 2 tablespoons avocado oil
- 1 cup water
- 2 radishes, ends trimmed, leaves rinsed and roughly chopped
- Freshly ground black pepper, to taste

**Directions:**

1. In a small bowl, mix the coriander, cumin, salt, paprika, and allspice. Rub the spice mixture all over the short ribs.
2. Set the Instant Pot to Sauté mode and add the oil to heat. Add the short ribs, bone side up. Brown for 4 minutes on each side.
3. Pour the water into the Instant Pot. Secure the lid. Press the Manual button and set cooking time for 45 minutes on High Pressure.
4. When timer beeps, allow the pressure to release naturally for 10 minutes, then release any remaining pressure. Open the lid.
5. Remove the short ribs to a serving plate.
6. Add the radishes to the sauce in the pot. Place a metal steaming basket directly on top of the radishes and place the radish leaves in the basket.
7. Secure the lid. Press the Manual button and set cooking time for 3 minutes on High Pressure.
8. When timer beeps, quick release the pressure. Open the lid. Transfer the leaves to a serving bowl. Sprinkle with salt and pepper.
9. Remove the radishes and place on top of the leaves. Serve hot with the short ribs.

## Nutrition:

Calories: 450

Fat: 24.8g

Protein: 45.4g

Carbs: 12.3g

Net carbs: 9.4g

Fiber: 2.9g

**Beef Shami Kabob**

**Preparation Time:** 15 minutes

**Cooking Time:** 35 minutes

**Servings:** 4

**Ingredients:**

- 1 pound (454 g) beef chunks, chopped
- 1 teaspoon ginger paste
- ½ teaspoon ground cumin
- 2 cups water
- ¼ cup almond flour
- 1 egg, beaten
- 1 tablespoon coconut oil

**Directions:**

1. Put the beef chunks, ginger paste, ground cumin, and water in the Instant Pot.
2. Select Manual mode and set cooking time for 30 minutes on High Pressure.
3. When timer beeps, make a quick pressure release. Open the lid.
4. Drain the water from the meat. Transfer the beef in the blender. Add the almond flour and beaten egg. Blend until smooth. Shape the mixture into small meatballs.
5. Heat the coconut oil on Sauté mode and put the meatballs inside.
6. Cook for 2 minutes on each side or until golden brown.
7. Serve immediately.

**Nutrition:**

Calories: 179                                       Fiber: 0.3g

Fat: 9.5g

Protein: 20.1g

Carbs: 2.9g

Net carbs: 2.6g

**Beef Shawarma and Veggie Salad Bowls**

**Preparation Time:** 10 minutes

**Cooking Time:** 19 minutes

**Servings:** 4

**Ingredients:**

- 2 teaspoons olive oil
- 1½ pounds (680 g) beef flank steak, thinly sliced
- Sea salt and freshly ground black pepper, to taste
- 1 teaspoon cayenne pepper
- ½ teaspoon ground bay leaf
- ½ teaspoon ground allspice
- ½ teaspoon cumin, divided
- ½ cup Greek yogurt
- 2 tablespoons sesame oil
- 1 tablespoon fresh lime juice
- 2 English cucumbers, chopped
- 1 cup cherry tomatoes, halved
- 1 red onion, thinly sliced
- ½ head romaine lettuce, chopped

**Directions:**

1. Press the Sauté button to heat up the Instant Pot. Then, heat the olive oil and cook the beef for about 4 minutes.
2. Add all seasonings, 1½ cups of water, and secure the lid.
3. Choose Manual mode. Set the cook time for 15 minutes on High Pressure.

4. Once cooking is complete, use a natural pressure release. Carefully remove the lid.
5. Allow the beef to cool completely.
6. To make the dressing, whisk Greek yogurt, sesame oil, and lime juice in a mixing bowl.
7. Then, divide cucumbers, tomatoes, red onion, and romaine lettuce among four serving bowls. Dress the salad and top with the reserved beef flank steak. Serve warm.

## Nutrition:

Calories: 367

Fat: 19.1g

Protein: 39.5g

Carbs: 8.4g

Net carbs: 5.0g

Fiber: 3.4g

## Beef Shoulder Roast

**Preparation Time:** 15 minutes

**Cooking Time:** 46 minutes

**Servings:** 6

## Ingredients:

- 2 tablespoons peanut oil
- 2 pounds (907 g) shoulder roast
- ¼ cup coconut aminos
- 1 teaspoon porcini powder
- 1 teaspoon garlic powder
- 1 cup beef broth
- 2 cloves garlic, minced
- 2 tablespoons champagne vinegar
- ½ teaspoon hot sauce
- 1 teaspoon celery seeds
- 1 cup purple onions, cut into wedges

- 1 tablespoon flaxseed meal, plus 2 tablespoons water

**Directions:**

1. Press the Sauté button to heat the Instant Pot. Then, heat the peanut oil and cook the beef shoulder roast for 3 minutes on each side.
2. In a mixing dish, combine coconut aminos, porcini powder, garlic powder, broth, garlic, vinegar, hot sauce, and celery seeds.
3. Pour the broth mixture into the Instant Pot. Add the onions to the top.
4. Secure the lid. Choose Meat/Stew mode and set cooking time for 40 minutes on High Pressure.
5. Once cooking is complete, use a natural pressure release for 15 minutes, then release any remaining pressure. Carefully remove the lid.
6. Make the slurry by mixing flaxseed meal with 2 tablespoons of water. Add the slurry to the Instant Pot.
7. Press the Sauté button and allow it to cook until the cooking liquid is reduced and thickened slightly. Serve warm.

**Nutrition:**

Calories: 313

Fat: 16.1g

Protein: 33.5g

Carbs: 6.5g

Net carbs: 3.1g

Fiber: 3.4g

**Beef Stuffed Kale Rolls**

**Preparation Time:** 15 minutes

**Cooking Time:** 30 minutes

**Servings:** 4

**Ingredients:**

- 8 ounces (227 g) ground beef
- 1 teaspoon chives
- ¼ teaspoon cayenne pepper
- 4 kale leaves

- 1 tablespoon cream cheese
- ¼ cup heavy cream
- ½ cup chicken broth

**Directions:**

1. In the mixing bowl, combine the ground beef, chives, and cayenne pepper.
2. Then fill and roll the kale leaves with ground beef mixture.
3. Place the kale rolls in the Instant Pot.
4. Add cream cheese, heavy cream, and chicken broth. Close the lid.
5. Select Manual mode and set cooking time for 30 minutes on High Pressure
6. When timer beeps, make a quick pressure release. Open the lid.
7. Serve warm.

**Nutrition:**

Calories: 153

Fat: 7.4g

Protein: 18.7g

Carbs: 2.2g

Net carbs: 1.9g

Fiber: 0.3g

**Beef, Bacon and Cauliflower Rice Casserole**

**Preparation Time:** 15 minutes

**Cooking Time:** 26 minutes

**Servings:** 5

**Ingredients:**

- 2 cups fresh cauliflower florets
- 1 pound (454 g) ground beef
- 5 slices uncooked bacon, chopped
- 8 ounces (227 g) unsweetened tomato puree
- 1 cup shredded Cheddar cheese, divided
- 1 teaspoon garlic powder

- ½ teaspoon paprika
- ½ teaspoon sea salt
- ¼ teaspoon ground black pepper
- ¼ teaspoon celery seed
- 1 cup water
- 1 medium Roma tomato, sliced

**Directions:**

1. Spray a round soufflé dish with coconut oil cooking spray. Set aside.
2. Add the cauliflower florets to a food processor and pulse until a riced. Set aside.
3. Select Sauté mode. Once the pot is hot, crumble the ground beef into the pot and add the bacon. Sauté for 6 minutes or until the ground beef is browned and the bacon is cooked through.
4. Transfer the beef, bacon, and rendered fat to a large bowl.
5. Add the cauliflower rice, tomato puree ½ cup Cheddar cheese, garlic powder, paprika, sea salt, black pepper, and celery seed to the bowl with the beef bacon. Mix well to combine.
6. Add the mixture to the prepared dish and use a spoon to press and smooth the mixture into an even layer.
7. Place the trivet in the Instant Pot and add the water to the bottom of the pot. Place the dish on top of the trivet.
8. Lock the lid. Select Manual mode and set cooking time for 20 minutes on High Pressure.
9. When cooking is complete, quick release the pressure.
10. Open the lid. Arrange the tomato slices in a single layer on top of the casserole and sprinkle the remaining cheese over top.
11. Secure the lid and let the residual heat melt the cheese for 5 minutes.
12. Open the lid, remove the dish from the pot.
13. Transfer the casserole to a serving plate and slice into 5 equal-sized wedges. Serve warm.

**Nutrition:**

Calories: 350

Fat: 22.7g

Protein: 30.0g

Carbs: 8.0g

Net carbs: 6.0g

Fiber: 2.0g

# Seafoods

## Salmon with Green Beans

**Preparation Time**: 10 minutes

**Cooking Time**: 20 minutes

**Servings**: 2

**Ingredients**

- 6 oz. green beans
- 3 oz. unsalted butter
- 2 salmon fillets
- Seasoning:
- ½ tsp garlic powder
- ½ tsp salt
- ½ tsp cracked black pepper

**Directions:**

1. Take a frying pan, place butter in it. When it starts to melts, add beans and salmon in fillets in it, season with garlic powder, salt, and black pepper, and cook for 8 minutes until salmon is cooked, turning halfway through and stirring the beans frequently.
2. When done, evenly divide salmon and green beans between two plates and serve.

**Nutrition**: 352 Calories; 29 g Fats; 19 g Protein; 3.5 g Net Carb; 1.5 g Fiber;

## Salmon Sheet pan

**Preparation Time**: 10 minutes

**Cooking Time**: 20 minutes

**Servings**: 2

### Ingredients

- 2 salmon fillets
- 2 oz. cauliflower florets
- 2 oz. broccoli florets
- 1 tsp minced garlic
- 1 tbsp. chopped cilantro
- Seasoning:
- 2 tbsp. coconut oil
- 2/3 tsp salt
- ¼ tsp ground black pepper

### Directions:

1. Turn on the oven, then set it to 400 degrees F, and let it preheat.
2. Place oil in a small bowl, add garlic and cilantro, stir well, and microwave for 1 minute or until the oil has melted.
3. Take a rimmed baking sheet, place cauliflower and broccoli florets in it, drizzle with 1 tbsp. of coconut oil mixture, season with 1/3 tsp salt, 1/8 tsp black pepper and bake for 10 minutes.
4. Then push the vegetables to a side, place salmon fillets in the pan, drizzle with remaining coconut oil mixture, season with remaining salt and black pepper on both sides and bake for 10 minutes until salmon is fork-tender.
5. Serve.

**Nutrition**: 450 Calories; 23.8 g Fats; 36.9 g Protein; 5.9 g Net Carb; 2.4 g Fiber;

## Fish with Kale and Olives

**Preparation Time**: 5 minutes

**Cooking Time**: 12 minutes;

**Servings**: 2

### Ingredients

- 2 pacific whitening fillets
- 2 oz. chopped kale
- 3 tbsp. coconut oil
- 2 scallion, chopped
- 6 green olives
- Seasoning:
- 1/2 tsp salt
- 1/3 tsp ground black pepper
- 3 drops of liquid stevia

### Directions:

1. Take a large skillet pan, place it over medium-high heat, add 4 tbsp. water, then add kale, toss and cook for 2 minutes until leaves are wilted but green.
2. When done, transfer kale to a strainer placed on a bowl and set aside until required.
3. Wipe clean the pan, add 2 tbsp. oil, and wait until it melts.
4. Season fillets with 1/3 tsp salt and ¼ tsp black pepper, place them into the pan skin-side up and cook for 4 minutes per side until fork tender.
5. Transfer fillets to a plate, add remaining oil to the pan, then add scallion and olives and cook for 1 minute.
6. Return kale into the pan, stir until mixed, cook for 1 minute until hot and then season with remaining salt and black pepper.
7. Divide kale mixture between two plates, top with cooked fillets, and then serve.

**Nutrition**: 454 Calories; 35.8 g Fats; 16 g Protein; 13.5 g Net Carb; 3.5 g Fiber;

## Cardamom Salmon

**Preparation Time**: 5 minutes

**Cooking Time**: 20 minutes

**Servings**: 2

**Ingredients**

- 2 salmon fillets
- ¾ tsp salt
- 2/3 tbsp. ground cardamom
- 1 tbsp. liquid stevia
- 1 ½ tbsp. avocado oil

**Directions:**

1. Turn on the oven, then set it to 275 degrees F and let it preheat.
2. Meanwhile, prepare the sauce and for this, place oil in a small bowl, and whisk in cardamom and stevia until combined.
3. Take a baking dish, place salmon in it, brush with prepared sauce on all sides, and let it marinate for 20 minutes at room temperature.
4. Then season salmon with salt and bake for 15 to 20 minutes until thoroughly cooked.
5. When done, flake salmon with two forks and then serve.

**Nutrition:** 143.3 Calories; 10.7 g Fats; 11.8 g Protein; 0 g Net Carb; 0 g Fiber;

## Garlic Butter Salmon

**Preparation Time**: 10 minutes

**Cooking Time**: 15 minutes

**Servings**: 2

**Ingredients**

- 2 salmon fillets, skinless
- 1 tsp minced garlic
- 1 tbsp. chopped cilantro
- 1 tbsp. unsalted butter
- 2 tbsp. grated cheddar cheese
- Seasoning:
- ½ tsp salt
- ¼ tsp ground black pepper

**Directions:**

1. Turn on the oven, then set it to 350 degrees F, and let it preheat.
2. Meanwhile, taking a rimmed baking sheet, grease it with oil, place salmon fillets on it, season with salt and black pepper on both sides.
3. Stir together butter, cilantro, and cheese until combined, then coat the mixture on both sides of salmon in an even layer and bake for 15 minutes until thoroughly cooked.
4. Turn on the broiler and continue baking the salmon for 2 minutes until the top is golden brown.
5. Serve.

**Nutrition:** 128 Calories; 4.5 g Fats; 41 g Protein; 1 g Net Carb; 0 g Fiber;

## Stir-fry Tuna with Vegetables

**Preparation Time**: 5 minutes;

**Cooking Time**: 15 minutes

**Servings**: 2

### Ingredients

- 4 oz. tuna, packed in water
- 2 oz. broccoli florets
- ½ of red bell pepper, cored, sliced
- ½ tsp minced garlic
- ½ tsp sesame seeds
- Seasoning:
- 1 tbsp. avocado oil
- 2/3 tsp soy sauce
- 2/3 tsp apple cider vinegar
- 3 tbsp. water

### Directions:

1. Take a skillet pan, add ½ tbsp. oil and when hot, add bell pepper and cook for 3 minutes until tender-crisp.
2. Then add broccoli floret, drizzle with water and continue cooking for 3 minutes until steamed, covering the pan.
3. Uncover the pan, cook for 2 minutes until all the liquid has evaporated, and then push bell pepper to one side of the pan.
4. Add remaining oil to the other side of the pan, add tuna and cook for 3 minutes until seared on all sides.
5. Then drizzle with soy sauce and vinegar, toss all the pan's ingredients until mixed and sprinkle with sesame seeds.
6. Serve.

**Nutrition**: 99.7 Calories; 5.1 g Fats; 11 g Protein; 1.6 g Net Carb; 1 g Fiber;

## Baked Fish with Feta and Tomato

**Preparation Time**: 5 minutes

**Cooking Time**: 15 minutes;

**Servings**: 2

**Ingredients**

- 2 pacific whitening fillets
- 1 scallion, chopped
- 1 Roma tomato, chopped
- 1 tsp fresh oregano
- 1-ounce feta cheese, crumbled
- Seasoning:
- 2 tbsp. avocado oil
- 1/3 tsp salt
- 1/4 tsp ground black pepper
- ¼ crushed red pepper

### Directions:

1. Turn on the oven, then set it to 400 degrees F and let it preheat.
2. Take a medium skillet pan, place it over medium heat, add oil, add scallion and cook for 3 minutes.
3. Add tomatoes, stir in ½ tsp oregano, 1/8 tsp salt, black pepper, red pepper, pour in ¼ cup water and bring it to simmer.
4. Sprinkle remaining salt over fillets, add to the pan, drizzle with remaining oil, and then bake for 10 to 12 minutes until fillets are fork-tender.
5. When done, top fish with remaining oregano and cheese and then serve.

**Nutrition**: 427.5 Calories; 29.5 g Fats; 26.7 g Protein; 8 g Net Carb; 4 g Fiber;

**Chili-glazed Salmon**

**Preparation Time**: 5 minutes

**Cooking Time**: 10 minutes

**Servings**: 2

**Ingredients**

- 2 salmon fillets
- 2 tbsp. sweet chili sauce
- 2 tsp chopped chives
- ½ tsp sesame seeds

**Directions:**

1. Turn on the oven, then set it to 400 degrees F and let it preheat.
2. Meanwhile, place salmon in a shallow dish, add chili sauce and chives and toss until mixed.
3. Transfer prepared salmon onto a baking sheet lined with parchment sheet, drizzle with remaining sauce and bake for 10 minutes until thoroughly cooked.
4. Garnish with sesame seeds and Serve.

**Nutrition**: 112.5 Calories; 5.6 g Fats; 12 g Protein; 3.4 g Net Carb; 0 g Fiber;

## Creamy Tuna, Spinach, and Eggs Plates

**Preparation Time**: 5 minutes

**Cooking Time**: 0 minutes;

**Servings**: 2

### Ingredients

- 2 oz. of spinach leaves
- 2 oz. tuna, packed in water
- 2 eggs, boiled
- 4 tbsp. cream cheese, full-fat
- Seasoning:
  - ¼ tsp salt
  - 1/8 tsp ground black pepper

### Directions:

1. Take two plates and evenly distribute spinach and tuna between them.
2. Peel the eggs, cut them into half, and divide them between the plates and then season with salt and black pepper.
3. Serve with cream cheese.

**Nutrition:** 212 Calories; 14.1 g Fats; 18 g Protein; 1.9 g Net Carb; 1.3 g Fiber;

## Tuna and Avocado

**Preparation Time**: 5 minutes;

**Cooking Time**: 0 minutes;

**Servings**: 2

### Ingredients

- 2 oz. tuna, packed in water
- 1 avocado, pitted
- 8 green olives
- ½ cup mayonnaise, full-fat
- Seasoning:
- 1/3 tsp salt
- 1/4 tsp ground black pepper

### Directions:

1. Cut avocado into half, then remove the pit, scoop out the flesh and distribute between two plates.
2. Add tuna and green olives and then season with salt and black pepper.
3. Serve with mayonnaise.

**Nutrition**: 680 Calories; 65.6 g Fats; 10.2 g Protein; 2.2 g Net Carb; 9.7 g Fiber;

## Garlic Oregano Fish

**Preparation Time**: 5 minutes

**Cooking Time**: 12 minutes;

**Servings**: 2

### Ingredients

- 2 pacific whitening fillets
- 1 tsp minced garlic
- 1 tbsp. butter, unsalted
- 2 tsp dried oregano
- Seasoning:
- 1/3 tsp salt
- 1/4 tsp ground black pepper

### Directions:

1. Turn on the oven, then set it to 400 degrees F and let it preheat.
2. Meanwhile, take a small saucepan, place it over low heat, add butter and when it melts, stir in garlic and cook for 1 minute, remove the pan from heat.
3. Season fillets with salt and black pepper, and place them on a baking dish greased with oil.
4. Pour butter mixture over fillets, then sprinkle with oregano and bake for 10 to 12 minutes until thoroughly cooked.
5. Serve.

**Nutrition**: 199.5 Calories; 7 g Fats; 33.5 g Protein; 0.9 g Net Carb; 0.1 g Fiber;

## Bacon wrapped Salmon

**Preparation Time**: 5 minutes

**Cooking Time**: 10 minutes

**Servings**: 2

**Ingredients**

- 2 salmon fillets, cut into four pieces
- 4 slices of bacon
- 2 tsp avocado oil
- 2 tbsp. mayonnaise
- Seasoning:
- ½ tsp salt
- ½ tsp ground black pepper

**Directions:**

1. Turn on the oven, then set it to 375 degrees F and let it preheat.
2. Meanwhile, place a skillet pan, place it over medium-high heat, add oil and let it heat.
3. Season salmon fillets with salt and black pepper, wrap each salmon fillet with a bacon slice, then add to the pan and cook for 4 minutes, turning halfway through.
4. Then transfer skillet pan containing salmon into the oven and cook salmon for 5 minutes until thoroughly cooked.
5. Serve salmon with mayonnaise

**Nutrition**: 190.7 Calories; 16.5 g Fats; 10.5 g Protein; 0 g Net Carb; 0 g Fiber;

## Fish and Spinach Plate

**Preparation Time**: 10 minutes

**Cooking Time**: 10 minutes;

**Servings**: 2

### Ingredients

- 2 pacific whitening fillets
- 2 oz. spinach
- ½ cup mayonnaise
- 1 tbsp. avocado oil
- 1 tbsp. unsalted butter
- Seasoning:
- 1/2 tsp salt
- 1/3 tsp ground black pepper

### Directions:

1. Take a frying pan, place it over medium heat, add butter and wait until it melts.
2. Season fillets with 1/3 tsp salt and ¼ tsp black pepper, add to the pan, and cook for 5 minutes per side until golden brown and thoroughly cooked.
3. Transfer fillets to two plates, distribute spinach among them, and drizzle with oil and season with remaining salt and black pepper.
4. Serve with mayonnaise.

**Nutrition**: 389 Calories; 34 g Fats; 7.7 g Protein; 10.6 g Net Carb; 2 g Fiber

## Fish and Egg Plate

**Preparation Time**: 5 minutes;

**Cooking Time**: 10 minutes;

**Servings**: 2

**Ingredients**

- 2 eggs
- 1 tbsp. butter, unsalted
- 2 pacific whitening fillets
- ½ oz. chopped lettuce
- 1 scallion, chopped
- Seasoning:
- 3 tbsp. avocado oil
- 1/3 tsp salt
- 1/3 tsp ground black pepper

**Directions:**

1. Cook the eggs and for this, take a frying pan, place it over medium heat, add butter and when it melts, crack the egg in the pan and cook for 2 to 3 minutes until fried to desired liking.
2. Transfer fried egg to a plate and then cook the remaining egg in the same manner.
3. Meanwhile, season fish fillets with ¼ tsp each of salt and black pepper.
4. When eggs have fried, sprinkle salt and black pepper on them, then add 1 tbsp. oil into the frying pan, add fillets and cook for 4 minutes per side until thoroughly cooked.
5. When done, distribute fillets to the plate, add lettuce and scallion, drizzle with remaining oil, and then serve.

# Snacks

## Blueberry Scones

**Preparation Time: 5 minutes**

**Cooking Time: 25 minutes**

**Servings: 2**

**Ingredients:**

- 2 cups almond flour
- 1/3 cup Swerve sweetener
- ¼ cup coconut flour
- 1 tbsp. baking powder
- ¼ tsp salt
- 2 large eggs
- ¼ cup heavy whipping cream
- ½ tsp vanilla extract
- ¾ cup fresh blueberries

**Directions:**

1. Preheat your oven at 325 degrees F. Layer a baking sheet with wax paper.
2. Whisk almond flour with baking powder, salt, coconut flour, and sweetener in a large bowl.
3. Stir in eggs, vanilla, and cream then mix well until fully incorporated.
4. Add blueberries and mix gently.
5. Spread this dough on a baking sheet and form it into a 10x8-inch rectangle.
6. Bake these scones for 25 minutes until golden.
7. Allow them to cool then serve.

**Nutrition:**

Calories: 266

Fat 25.7 g

Saturated Fat 1.2 g

Cholesterol 41

Sodium 18

# Homemade Graham Crackers

**Preparation Time: 5 minutes**

**Cooking Time: 30 minutes**

**Servings: 12**

**Ingredients:**

- 2 cups almond flour
- 1/3 cup Swerve Brown
- 2 tsp cinnamon
- 1 tsp baking powder
- Pinch salt
- 1 large egg
- 2 tbsp. butter, melted
- 1 tsp vanilla extract

**Directions:**

1. Preheat your oven at 300 degrees F.
2. Whisk almond flour, baking powder, salt, cinnamon, and sweetener in a large bowl.
3. Stir in melted butter, egg, and vanilla extract.
4. Mix well to form the dough then spread it out into a ¼-inch thick sheet.
5. Slice the sheet into 2x2-inch squares and place them on a baking sheet with wax paper.
6. Bake them for 30 minutes until golden then let them sit for 30 minutes at room temperature until cooled.
7. Break the crackers into smaller squares and put them back in the hot oven for 30 minutes. Keep the oven off during this time.
8. Enjoy.

**Nutrition:**

Calories: 243

Fat: 21 g

Cholesterol: 121

Sodium: 34

Carb0hydrates: 7.3

Protein: 4.3 g

## Buffalo Chicken Sausage Balls

**Preparation Time: 5 minutes**

**Cooking Time: 25 minutes**

**Servings: 2**

**Ingredients:**

- Sausage Balls:
- 2 14-ox sausages, casings removed
- 2 cups almond flour
- 1 ½ cups shredded cheddar cheese
- ½ cup crumbled bleu cheese
- 1 tsp salt
- ½ tsp pepper
- Bleu Cheese Ranch Dipping Sauce:
- 1/3 cup mayonnaise
- 1/3 cup almond milk, unsweetened
- 2 cloves garlic, minced
- 1 tsp dried dill
- ½ tsp dried parsley
- ½ tsp salt
- ½ tsp pepper
- ¼ cup crumbled bleu cheese (or more, if desired)

**Directions:**

1. Preheat your oven at 35o degrees F.
2. Layer two baking sheets with wax paper and set them aside.
3. Mix sausage with cheddar cheese, almond flour, salt, pepper, and bleu cheese in a large bowl.
4. Make 1-inch balls out of this mixture and place them on the baking sheets.
5. Bake them for 25 minutes until golden brown.
6. Meanwhile, prepare the dipping sauce by whisking all of its ingredients in a bowl.
7. Serve the balls with this dipping sauce.

## Nutrition:

Calories: 183

Fat: 15 g

Cholesterol 11 mg

Sodium 31 mg

Total carbohydrates 6.2 g

Protein 4.5 g

## Brussels Sprouts Chips

## Preparation Time: 5 minutes

## Cooking Time: 15 minutes

## Servings: 6

## Ingredients:

- 1-pound Brussels sprouts, washed and dried
- 2 tbsp. extra virgin olive oil
- 1 tsp kosher salt

## Directions:

1. Preheat your oven at 400 degrees F.
2. After peeling the sprouts off the stem, discard the outer leaves of the Brussel sprouts.
3. Separate all the leaves from one another and place them on a baking sheet.
4. Toss them with oil and salt thoroughly to coat them well.
5. Spread the leaves out on two greased baking sheets then bake them for 15 minutes until crispy.
6. Serve.

## Nutrition:

Calories: 188

Fat: 3 g

Cholesterol: 101

Sodium: 54 mg

Fiber 0.6 g

Protein 5 g

## Keto Chocolate Mousse

**Preparation Time: 5 minutes**

**Cooking Time: 0 minutes**

**Servings: 2**

**Ingredients:**

- 1 cup heavy whipping cream
- ¼ cup unsweetened cocoa powder, sifted
- ¼ cup Swerve powdered sweetener
- 1 tsp vanilla extract
- ¼ tsp kosher salt

**Directions:**

1. Add cream to the bowl of an electric stand mixture and beat it until it forms peaks.
2. Stir in cocoa powder, vanilla, sweetener, and salt.
3. Mix well until smooth.
4. Refrigerate for 4 hours.
5. Serve.

**Nutrition:**

Calories: 153

Fat: 13 g

Cholesterol: 6.5 mg

Sodium: 81 mg

Sugar 1.4 g

Protein 5.8 g

**Keto Berry Mousse**

**Preparation Time: 5 minutes**

**Cooking Time: 0 minutes**

**Servings: 2**

**Ingredients:**

- 2 cups heavy whipping cream
- 3 oz. fresh raspberries
- 2 oz. chopped pecans
- ½ lemon, zested
- ¼ tsp vanilla extract

**Directions:**

1. Beat cream in a bowl using a hand mixer until it forms peaks.
2. Stir in vanilla and lemon zest and mix well until incorporated.
3. Fold in nuts and berries and mix well.
4. Cover the mixture with plastic wrap and refrigerate for 3 hours.
5. Serve fresh.

**Nutrition:**

Calories: 254

Fat: 9 g

Cholesterol: 13 mg

Sodium: 179 mg

Sugar 1.2 g

Protein 7.5 g

# Peanut Butter Mousse

**Preparation Time: 5 minutes**

**Cooking Time: 0 minutes**

**Servings: 4**

**Ingredients:**

- ½ cup heavy whipping cream
- 4 oz. cream cheese, softened
- ¼ cup natural peanut butter
- ¼ cup powdered Swerve sweetener
- ½ tsp vanilla extract

**Direction:**

1. Beat ½ cup cream in a medium bowl with a hand mixer until it forms peaks.
2. Beat cream cheese with peanut butter in another bowl until creamy.
3. Stir in vanilla, a pinch of salt, and sweetener to the peanut butter mix and combine until smooth.
4. Fold in the prepared whipped cream and mix well until fully incorporated.
5. Divide the mousse into 4 serving glasses.
6. Garnish as desired.
7. Enjoy.

**Nutrition:**

Calories: 290

Fat: 21.5

Cholesterol: 12

Sodium: 9

Protein: 6

# Cookie Ice Cream

**Preparation Time: 10 minutes**

**Cooking Time: 120 minutes**

**Servings: 2**

**Ingredients:**

- Cookie Crumbs
- ¾ cup almond flour
- ¼ cup cocoa powder
- ¼ tsp baking soda
- ¼ cup erythritol
- ½ tsp vanilla extract
- 1 ½ tbsp. coconut oil, softened
- 1 large egg, room temperature
- Pinch of salt
- Ice Cream
- 2 ½ cups whipping cream
- 1 tbsp. vanilla extract
- ½ cup erythritol
- ½ cup almond milk, unsweetened

**Directions:**

1. Preheat your oven at 300 degrees F and layer a 9-inch baking pan with wax paper.
2. Whisk almond flour with baking soda, cocoa powder, salt, and erythritol in a medium bowl.
3. Stir in coconut oil and vanilla extract then mix well until crumbly.
4. Whisk in egg and mix well to form the dough.
5. Spread this dough in the prepared pan and bake for 20 minutes in the preheated oven.
6. Allow the crust to cool then crush it finely into crumbles.
7. Beat cream in a large bowl with a hand mixer until it forms a stiff peak.
8. Stir in erythritol and vanilla extract then mix well until fully incorporated.
9. Pour in milk and blend well until smooth.
10. Add this mixture to an ice cream machine and churn as per the machine's instructions.

11.  Add cookie crumbles to the ice cream in the machine and churn again.
12.  Place the ice cream in a sealable container and freeze for 2 hours.
13.  Scoop out the ice cream and serve.
14.  Enjoy.
15.  *Note:* this recipe calls for an ice cream machine

**Nutrition:**

Calories: 214

Fat: 19

Cholesterol: 15

Sodium: 12

Fiber: 2

Protein: 7

## Mocha Ice Cream

**Preparation Time: 10 minutes**

**Cooking Time: 0 minutes**

**Servings: 2**

**Ingredients:**

- 1 cup coconut milk
- ¼ cup heavy whipping cream
- 2 tbsp. erythritol
- 15 drops liquid stevia
- 2 tbsp. unsweetened cocoa powder
- 1 tbsp. instant coffee
- ¼ tsp xanthan gum

**Directions:**

1. Whisk everything except xanthan gum in a bowl using a hand mixer.
2. Slowly add xanthan gum and stir well to make a thick mixture.
3. Churn the mixture in an ice cream machine as per the machine's instructions.
4. Freeze it for 2 hours then garnish with mint and instant coffee.
5. Serve.

6. *Note:* this recipe calls for an ice cream machine

## Nutrition:

Calories: 267

Fat: 44.5 g

Cholesterol: 153 mg

Sodium: 217 mg

## Raspberry Cream Fat Bombs
## Preparation Time: 10 minutes
## Cooking Time: 0 minutes
## Servings: 2
## Ingredients:

- 1 packet raspberry Jello (sugar-free)
- 1 tsp gelatin powder
- ½ cup of boiling water
- ½ cup heavy cream

## Directions:

1. Mix Jello and gelatin in boiling water in a medium bowl.
2. Stir in cream slowly and mix it for 1 minute.
3. Divide this mixture into candy molds.
4. Refrigerate them for 30 minutes.
5. Enjoy.

## Nutrition:

Calories: 197

Fat: 19.2 g

Cholesterol: 11 mg

Sodium: 78 mg

# Cauliflower Tartar Bread

**Preparation Time: 10 minutes**

**Cooking Time: 50 minutes**

**Servings: 4**

**Ingredients:**

- 3 cup cauliflower rice
- 10 large eggs, yolks and egg whites separated
- ¼ tsp cream of tartar
- 1 ¼ cup coconut flour
- 1 ½ tbsp. gluten-free baking powder
- 1 tsp sea salt
- 6 tbsp. butter
- 6 cloves garlic, minced
- 1 tbsp. fresh rosemary, chopped
- 1 tbsp. fresh parsley, chopped

**Directions:**

1. Preheat your oven to 350 degrees F. Layer a 9x5-inch pan with wax paper.
2. Place the cauliflower rice in a suitable bowl and then cover it with plastic wrap.
3. Heat it for 4 minutes in the microwave. Heat more if the cauliflower isn't soft enough.
4. Place the cauliflower rice in a kitchen towel and squeeze it to drain excess water.
5. Transfer drained cauliflower rice to a food processor.
6. Add coconut flour, sea salt, baking powder, butter, egg yolks, and garlic. Blend until crumbly.
7. Beat egg whites with cream of tartar in a bowl until foamy.
8. Add egg white mixture to the cauliflower mixture and stir well with a spatula.
9. Fold in rosemary and parsley.
10. Spread this batter in the prepared baking pan evenly.
11. Bake it for 50 minutes until golden then allow it to cool.

**Nutrition:**

Calories: 104                          Carbohydrates: 4.7 g

Fat: 8.9 g

Cholesterol: 57 mg

Sodium: 340 mg

## Buttery Skillet Flatbread

## Preparation Time: 10 minutes

## Cooking Time: 10 minutes

## Servings: 4

## Ingredients:

- 1 cup almond flour
- 2 tbsp. coconut flour
- 2 tsp xanthan gum
- ½ tsp baking powder
- ½ tsp salt
- 1 whole egg + 1 egg white
- 1 tbsp. water (if needed)
- 1 tbsp. oil, for frying
- 1 tbsp. melted butter, for brushing

## Directions:

1. Mix xanthan gum with flours, salt, and baking powder in a suitable bowl.
2. Beat egg and egg white in a separate bowl then stir in the flour mixture.
3. Mix well until smooth. Add a tablespoon of water if the dough is too thick.
4. Place a large skillet over medium heat and heat oil.

## Nutrition:

Calories: 272

Fat: 18

Cholesterol: 6.1

**Fluffy Bites**

**Preparation Time: 20 minutes**

**Cooking Time: 60 minutes**

**Servings: 12**

**Ingredients:**

- 2 Teaspoons Cinnamon
- 2/3 Cup Sour Cream
- 2 Cups Heavy Cream
- 1 Teaspoon Scraped Vanilla Bean
- ¼ Teaspoon Cardamom
- 4 Egg Yolks
- Stevia to Taste

**Directions:**

1. Start by whisking your egg yolks until creamy and smooth.
2. Get out a double boiler, and add your eggs with the rest of your ingredients. Mix well.
3. Remove from heat, allowing it to cool until it reaches room temperature.
4. Refrigerate for an hour before whisking well.
5. Pour into molds, and freeze for at least an hour before serving.

**Nutrition:**

Calories: 363

Protein: 2

Fat: 40

Carbohydrates: 1

**Coconut Fudge**

**Preparation Time: 20 minutes**

**Cooking Time: 60 minutes**

**Servings: 12**

**Ingredients:**

- 2 Cups Coconut Oil
- ½ Cup Dark Cocoa Powder
- ½ Cup Coconut Cream
- ¼ Cup Almonds, Chopped
- ¼ Cup Coconut, Shredded
- 1 Teaspoon Almond Extract
- Pinch of Salt
- Stevia to Taste

**Directions:**

1. Pour your coconut oil and coconut cream in a bowl, whisking with an electric beater until smooth. Once the mixture becomes smooth and glossy, do not continue.
2. Begin to add in your cocoa powder while mixing slowly, making sure that there aren't any lumps.
3. Add in the rest of your ingredients, and mix well.
4. Line a bread pan with parchment paper, and freeze until it sets.
5. Slice into squares before serving.

**Nutrition:**

Calories: 172

Fat: 20

Carbohydrates: 3

# Nutmeg Nougat

**Preparation Time: 30 minutes**

**Cooking Time: 60 minutes**

**Servings: 12**

**Ingredients:**

- 1 Cup Heavy Cream
- 1 Cup Cashew Butter
- 1 Cup Coconut, Shredded
- ½ Teaspoon Nutmeg
- 1 Teaspoon Vanilla Extract, Pure
- Stevia to Taste

**Directions:**

1. Melt your cashew butter using a double boiler, and then stir in your vanilla extract, dairy cream, nutmeg and stevia. Make sure it's mixed well.
2. Remove from heat, allowing it to cooldown before refrigerating it for a half hour.
3. Shape into balls, and coat with shredded coconut. Chill for at least two hours before serving.

**Nutrition:**

Calories: 341

Fat: 34

Carbohydrates: 5

**Sweet Almond Bites**

**Preparation Time: 30 minutes**

**Cooking Time: 90 minutes**

**Servings: 12**

**Ingredients:**

- 18 Ounces Butter, Grass Fed
- 2 Ounces Heavy Cream
- ½ Cup Stevia
- 2/3 Cup Cocoa Powder
- 1 Teaspoon Vanilla Extract, Pure
- 4 Tablespoons Almond Butter

**Direction:**

1. Use a double boiler to melt your butter before adding in all of your remaining ingredients.
2. Place the mixture into molds, freezing for two hours before serving.

**Nutrition:**

Calories: 350

Protein: 2

Fat: 38

**Strawberry Cheesecake Minis**

**Preparation Time: 30 minutes**

**Cooking Time: 120 minutes**

**Servings: 12**

**Ingredients:**

- 1 Cup Coconut Oil
- 1 Cup Coconut Butter
- ½ Cup Strawberries, Sliced
- ½ Teaspoon Lime Juice
- 2 Tablespoons Cream Cheese, Full Fat

- Stevia to Taste

**Directions:**

1. Blend your strawberries.
2. Soften your cream cheese, and then add in your coconut butter.
3. Combine all ingredients, and then pour your mixture into silicone molds.
4. Freeze for at least two hours before serving.

**Nutrition:**

Calories: 372

Protein: 1

Fat: 41

Carbohydrates: 2

**Cocoa Brownies**

**Preparation Time: 10 minutes**

**Cooking Time: 30 minutes**

**Servings: 12**

**Ingredients:**

- 1 Egg
- 2 Tablespoons Butter, Grass Fed
- 2 Teaspoons Vanilla Extract, Pure
- ¼ Teaspoon Baking Powder
- ¼ Cup Cocoa Powder
- 1/3 Cup Heavy Cream
- ¾ Cup Almond Butter
- Pinch Sea Salt

**Directions:**

1. Break your egg into a bowl, whisking until smooth.
2. Add in all of your wet ingredients, mixing well.
3. Mix all dry ingredients into a bowl.

4. Sift your dry ingredients into your wet ingredients, mixing to form a batter.
5. Get out a baking pan, greasing it before pouring in your mixture.
6. Heat your oven to 350 and bake for twenty-five minutes.
7. Allow it to cool before slicing and serve room temperature or warm.

## Nutrition:

Calories: 184

Protein: 1

Fat: 20

Carbohydrates: 1

# Conclusion

Start with non-processed carbs like whole grain, beans, and fruits. Start slow and see how your body responds before resolving to add carbs one meal at a time.

The things to watch out for when coming off keto are weight gain, bloating, more energy, and feeling hungry. The weight gain is nothing to freak out over; perhaps, you might not even gain any. It all depends on your diet, how your body processes carbs, and, of course, water weight. The length of your keto diet is a significant factor in how much weight you have lost, caused by the reduction of carbs. The bloating will occur because of the reintroduction of fibrous foods and your body getting used to digesting them again. The bloating van lasts for a few days to a few weeks. You will feel like you have more energy because carbs break down into glucose, the body's primary fuel source. You may also notice better brain function and the ability to work out more.

The ketogenic diet is the ultimate tool you can use to plan your future. Can you picture being more involved, more productive and efficient, and more relaxed and energetic? That future is possible for you, and it does not have to be a complicated process to achieve that vision. You can choose right now to be healthier and slimmer and more fulfilled tomorrow. It is possible with the ketogenic diet.

This is not a fancy diet that promises falsehoods of miracle weight loss. This diet is proven by years of science and research, which benefits your waistline and your heart, skin, brain, and organs. It does not just improve your physical health but your mental and emotional health as well. This diet improves your health holistically.

Keto diet provides long term health benefits compare to other diet plans. During keto diet near about 75 to 90 percent of calories comes from fats, an adequate number of calories 5 to 20 percent comes from proteins and 5 percent of calories from carb intake.

What began as a simple spark of curiosity ended on a high note: keto, a term you constantly read and heard about. Now you have all the knowledge in the world to lead a lifestyle that is truly worthy of your time, energy, and effort.

Whether you have met your weight loss goals, your life changes, or you simply want to eat whatever you want again. You cannot just suddenly start consuming carbs again for it will shock your system. Have an idea of what you want to allow back into your consumption slowly. Be familiar with portion sizes and stick to that amount of carbs for the first few times you eat post-keto.

Being 50 years old or more is not bad. It is how we handle ourselves in this age that matters. Most of us would have just moved on and dealt with things as they would have arrived. That is no longer the case. It is quite literally survival of the fittest.

Do not give up now as there will be quite a few days where you may think to yourself, "Why am I doing this?" and to answer that, simply focus on the goals you wish to achieve.

A good diet enriched with all the proper nutrients is our best shot of achieving an active metabolism and efficient lifestyle. Many people think that the Keto diet is simply for people interested in losing weight. You will find that it is quite the opposite. There are intense keto diets where only 5 percent of the diet comes from carbs, 20 percent is from protein, and 75 percent is from fat. But even a modified version of this which involves consciously choosing foods low in carbohydrate and high in healthy fats is good enough.

Made in the USA
Middletown, DE
27 April 2022

64829622R00144